Banking Success Factors Analysis

Gary P. Tobar

Abstract

Sawla Microfinance's 2019-2023 financial and non-financial performance highlights how banking industries can transition from microfinance to corporate banking. This research examines the relationship between proxy measures of business agility, lean banking, corporate social responsibility initiatives, and banking performance. A Kendall's Tau Correlational research design was implemented, encompassing a panel of quarterly data mined and records reviewed from Sawla District Omo Bank using purposive sampling. Due to the non-normal data distribution, a Kendall's Tau correlation was employed to test the existence of a statistically significant relationship, direction, and strength of monotonic nonlinear association among continuous variables. The result revealed a statistically positive significant correlation between the number of women loan beneficiaries and the number of depositors ($\tau=0.6962$, $p\leq0.0001$), number of loanees ($\tau=0.3636$, $p\leq0.05$), and return on asset ($\tau=0.5782$, $p\leq0.0001$). The finding explains how a higher investment in corporate social responsibility initiatives is associated with a higher customer and financial dimension. The findings showed a statistically positive significant correlation between cash flow and return on asset ($\tau=0.3471$, $p\leq0.05$) and number of depositors ($\tau=0.3824$, $p\leq0.05$). The result implies that a higher cash flow correlates with a higher return on assets and a higher savings deposit to have sufficient financial capability to mitigate challenges in an agile banking business. The result unveiled a statistically positive significant correlation between loan repaid and business process ($\tau=0.4106$, $p\leq0.05$), implying that as loan repaid increases, the business process improves.

Acknowledgments

First and foremost, I want to thank God for guiding me to this incredible

achievement. His unwavering support led me to success and gave me hope during tough

times. The Virgin Mary and Saint Arsema, thank you for your comforting presence and

intercession. I also cannot forget to mention my guardian angel, Gabriel, who has been

watching over me since day one.

To Dr. Ryan Tipton, my committee chair, your invaluable guidance was crucial in

my doctoral pursuit. Thank you to the committee members Dr. Brianna Lopez, Dr. David

Arnold, Dr. Sandra Johnson, and program directors Sarah Krohn and Sandy Wilkinson

for your unwavering support.

To my beloved parents, Azenegash and Ambaye, your blessings and prayers have

been instrumental in my journey. I am also grateful for the prayers of my spiritual fathers,

Abuna Markos, Abuna Abraham, Fr. Haddis, Fr. Menkir, and Fr. Kibru.

To my dear wife, Nigatuwa, your prayer was my strength. To my cherished

daughter Eleni, you inspire me every day. To all my beloved family members, friends,

and EOTC church communities - Sawla Menberetsehay, Lynnwood Anketse Birhan,

Seattle Mekanebirhan, Debre Bisrat, Micheal's family, Fr. Nebiyat's family, and many

others - your encouragement has been an immense source of motivation. I am profoundly

grateful for your unwavering support throughout my doctoral studies.

To my dear brothers – Dr. Shimelis, Abinet, Tegenne, Dawit, Abraham,

Tegegnwork, Wudineh, Habtamu, Mihreteab, Mekuwanint, Wandimagegn, Dagmawi,

Sofoniyas, Aman, Yohanes, and all others – your friendship meant everything. Thank you

all for being part of my journey, and may God abundantly bless each of you.

Table of Contents

List of Tables vii

List of Figures viii

Chapter 1: Foundations of the Study...1

Background of the Problem 2

Problem Statement 3

Purpose Statement.. 4

Nature of the Study 6

Research Questions.. 7

Hypotheses 8

Theoretical Framework... 9

David Teece, Gary Pisano, and Amy Shuen's Theory of Dynamic Capabilities and

Strategic Management 10

James Womack and Daniel Jones's Theory of Lean Management................................. 10

Howard Bowen and Archie Carroll's Theory of Social Responsibility 11

Operational Definitions... 11

Assumptions, Limitations, and Delimitations... 13

Assumptions... 13

Limitations 14

Delimitations... 15

Significance of the Study 15

Transition and Summary 16

Chapter 2: Review of the Professional and Academic Literature 18

Literature Search Strategy 18

Content of The Literature 18

The Organization of The Review 20

The Strategy for Searching the Literature 20

Peer-Reviewed Sources and Current References 21

Balanced Scorecard 23

Agile And Lean Leadership 28

Corporate Social Responsibility 28

Literature Review on Key Concepts and Variables 29

High Performance, Organizational Success, and Sustainability 29

Success Metrics and Dimensions of Organizational Performance of Banking 32

Financial Metrics 33

Return on Asset (ROA) 34

Return on Equity (ROE) 34

Operating Self-Sufficiency (OSS) 35

Portfolio at Risk (PAR) (> 30 days) 35

The Ratio of Operating Expense to Loan Portfolio (OE/LP) 36

Customer Dimension Metrics 36

Customer Satisfaction Using the Likert Scale 37

Customer Retention Using Percentage Change 38

Internal Business Process Dimension Metrics 38

Cycle Time: Duration of Loan Application Processing 39

Borrowers Per Loan Officers: Proxy of Operational Efficiency 40

Learning and Growth Dimension Metrics 41

Employee Satisfaction: Employee Turnover Rate 43

Investment in Information Systems and Information Technology 44

Corporate Social Responsibility (CSR) Dimensions and Corporate Social Performance

(CSP) Metrics 44

Investment in Initiatives of Environment, Social, and Governance (ESG) 47

Financial and Social Inclusion: Percentage of Population Served and Vulnerable

Population Served 48

Business Agility Metrics 52

Dimensions of Agility and Cash Flow as A Proxy Measure 54

Lean Banking Metrics 59

Cost-to-Income Ratio 60

Operational Efficiency: Percentage of Loan Repaid 61

Predictive Modeling and Research Analysis in Business 64

The Role and Application of Forecasting in Business 67

Summary and Transition 71

Chapter 3: Research Method and Design 72

Purpose Statement 72

Role of the Researcher 73

Participants 74

Research Method 78

Research Design 79

Population and Sampling 79

Ethical Research 82

Data Collection Instruments 83

Data Collection Technique 87

Data Analysis 87

Study Validity 91

Transition and Summary 93

Chapter 4: Results 95

Data Collection 97

Reliability and Validity 98

Data Analysis 99

Results 100

Distribution of the Data 104

Testing for Existence of Significance 109

Testing for Direction and Strength of Relationship 112

Transition and Summary 115

Chapter 5: Discussion, Conclusions, and Recommendations 116

Interpretation of the Findings 116

Key Findings 118

Relationship Between the Proxy Measures of CSR And BSC Dimensions 118

Relationship Between the Proxy Measures of Business Agility and BSC Dimensions 120

Relationship Between the Proxy Measures of Lean Banking and BSC Dimensions ... 121

Limitations of the Study 122

Applications to Professional Practice 123

Implications for Social Change 124

Recommendations for Action 125

Scale Up Women's Financial Inclusion and Work on Savings for Financial Capability .. 125

Increase Loan Repayment for Improved Business Processes and Lean Management 126

Disseminate The Research Result and Develop Scientific Approaches for Improved

Performance 126

Recommendations for Further Research 127

Identify Uncovered Proxy Measures 127

Expand Sample Size 128

Use Experimental Research 128

Reflections 129

Conclusion 129

List of Tables

Table 1. Audit of References 23

Table 2. Latent and Observed Variables 85

Table 3. Compact Table of Summary Statistics: Quartiles for Checking Outliers 101

Table 4. Compact Table of Summary Statistics: Measures of Central Tendency and

Dispersion 103

Table 5. Shapiro-Wilk Test for Normal Data 107

Table 6. Kendall's Tau Correlation Matrix 109

List of Figures

Figure 1. Sample Location Map...77

Figure 2. Approximately Normally Distributed Variables 105

Figure 3. Non-Normal Variables: Right Skewed...106

Figure 4. Non-Normal Variables: Left Skewed...106

Chapter 1: Foundations of the Study

Self-sufficiency and sustainability of businesses are among the areas of attention of organizational performance and strategic management scholars. Microfinance industries are a means to support sustainable development goals in reducing world poverty growth by delivering financial services to people experiencing poverty (Wadi et al., 2021). Though there are still debates on whether sustainability is a strategic differentiator for organizational performance or a necessity, Ioannou and Serafeim (2019) contend that sustainability is necessary for realizing a business's longevity and a differentiator in the era of the digital and competitive market of corporate industries. From a business point of view, meeting financial sustainability and self-sufficiency have been a challenge in Sub-Saharan African (SSA) microfinance banking industries (Remer & Kattilakoski, 2021; Tehulu, 2022).

Like the times of woes, good times wowed business scholars of banking industries (Kempner, 2012; Schlein, 2021). The success and failures of microfinance banking industries are not solely attached to financial performance. However, operational and non-financial performance significantly contributed to the sustainability and self-sufficiency of banking firms. Developing nations' microfinance is at the infant stage of adopting and implementing a proper strategic management tool to realize sustainable firms (Refera, 2020). Besides, the ever-changing business environment is putting the predictability of business sustainability in danger. Hence, such challenges call for further exploration of the relationship between business agility, organizational leanness, corporate social responsibility, and the Balanced Scorecard dimensions of finance, customer service, business process, and business learning and growth. If statistically significant relations prevail, testing for the direction and strength of the relationship is crucial to act on emerging predictors of banking performance and proactively mitigate unforeseen challenges.

Background of the Problem

The formal establishment of microfinance practices goes back to the foundation of the pawn shop in 1462 as a lending store by an Italian monk (Helms, 2006). Pope Leon X allowed Pawn Shops to charge an interest rate to cover operating expenses in 1515. Later in the 1990s, as microcredits expanded, microfinance increased its outreach and provided saving services. A recent study on 105 institutions found that the self-sufficiency challenge of microfinance outweighs nonprofits (Mumi et al., 2020).

A correlation study on the performance of microfinance analyzes associating the challenge of self-sufficiency with a lower interest rate (Ibrahim et al., 2018). The researchers contended that microfinance has reduced self-sufficiency potential due to a lower interest rate not enabling operational expenses. However, the analysis fails to consider the non-financial dimension contributing to a lag in performance. Conversely, researchers such as Ghosh and Guha (2019) found that clients and human resource dimensions affected the performance of 104 microfinance institutions in India.

Based on the descriptive statistics analysis undertaken on the open dataset of the MIX (Microfinance Exchange) Market on World Bank (2019), the world average record informs that the self-sufficiency ratio is 116% (1.16), indicating a break-even point with a "normal" balance of revenue and expenses. However, the Ethiopian Omo Microfinance, one of the Sub-Saharan microfinance industry's Operational Self-Sufficiency (OSS), is below the average world OSS by 3%. Hence, this calls for future research to comprehensively examine the financial and non-financial determinants leading to a below-average OSS in the microfinance industry. Besides, there is a need for an extensive research study using a Balanced Scorecard approach to identify a strategic managerial solution to improve self-sufficiency and performance lag, focusing on Southern Ethiopia Omo Microfinance.

Problem Statement

Microfinance institutions in Sub-Saharan Africa face a challenge in meeting operational self-sufficiency (Remer & Kattilakoski, 2021). In the empirical analysis of 416 micro-microfinance institutions, Laxmi and Hanna (2021) claim that return on asset, the ratio of total expense to assets, and financial revenue to asset determine the sustainability of microfinance. Looking at the MIX (Microfinance Exchange) Market data trend on World Bank (2019) from 1999 to 2019, the average Return on Assets (ROA) is 2.4% (below 5%), which indicates a lower profitability ratio. Simultaneously, according to the recent report from MIX, the OSS and ROA follow the same pattern with a significant positive relationship with an R-squared value of 0.119 and a P-value less than 0.0001 in the fiscal years 1999 -2019. As Gallo (2016) stated, Knight generally agrees that the profitability ratio should be as high as possible. However, the Microfinance (MF) industries are not meeting profitability objectives.

The extent of outreach also influences the institution's performance and social responsibility (Amidou et al., 2022; Awaworyi, 2020; Liu, 2021). For Wondimu (2020), procedural gaps during the lending process led to the loss of microfinance institutions. However, Md and Win (2020) relate the issue to the failure of the governance of microfinance. Accordingly, leaders' inflexibility and fragility to introduce innovative ideas impacted the efficacy of microfinance (Ahmad et al., 2019).

There are different arguments on mediating and moderating factors. The general problem is that a Balanced Scorecard (BSC) approach to measuring strategic and key performance indicators is at its infant adoption stage in Omo Microfinance in Ethiopia (Refera, 2020). Existing literature, such as Kaplan and Norton (2007), covered little about how business agility and leanness and Corporate Social Responsibility (CSR) have a relationship with the four BSC dimensions (customer, finance, learning and growth, and business process). Hence, the specific problem is that there needs to be more research undertaken to employ extended BSC, considering the influence of business agility and leanness and CSR initiatives in showing the challenge of self-sufficiency in the microfinance industry.

Purpose Statement

The purpose of this study was two-fold. The primary purpose was to assess and test the relationship between business agility and leanness, CSR practice, and the BSC dimensions: customer, financial, learning and growth, and business process. If a relationship exists, the study would further test the strength and direction of the relationship to establish comprehensive extended performance metrics and help future researchers build a predictive model to track the performance of the Omo microfinance institution. The study targets Omo Bank in southern Ethiopia, focusing on ten branches of Sawla Omo microfinance at the Gofa Zone administration. The study tries to identify and examine additional variables associated with microfinance performance and the challenge of self-sufficiency. The variables included are the observed variables associated with the four dimensions of BSC: business agility, leanness, and Corporate Social Responsibility (CSR). The observed variables for the latent or unobserved variables include Operating Self-Sufficiency (OSS), Return on Asset (ROA), Number of Depositors (CSSV) and Number of Loanee (CSLn), Number of New Borrowers (B), Number of Loan Officers (LnO), Employment Turnover Rate (ETR), Number of Women Loan Beneficiaries (WPn), Cash Flow (CshF) and Loan Repaid (LnRd). Based on theoretical literature, OSS depends on all the remaining explanatory variables.

The study used a quantitative research method. The study participants, the managerial bodies, and the employees working on the banking system extracted existing data from the internal database. The researcher worked on mining relevant variables to examine the trends and relationships among the selected variables. Moreover, the study encompassed quantitative operational and financial data trends within the recent five years, from 2019 to 2023. A correlational research design was used to conduct the study. The study incorporates a longitudinal dataset (Goldberger, 1972). Hence, the correlational research design suits studies interested in understanding the strength and direction of relationships among variables (Cho et al., 2022; Hair & Sarstedt, 2019; Zyphur et al., 2022). The study identifies how banking industries play a substantial role in the financial inclusion of women and other vulnerable parts of the community for the benefit of organizational performance and stewardship initiatives. Besides, the study provided insights and knowledge on how banking participation in corporate social responsibility, business agility, and lean banking pave the way for the success of the banking industry.

Nature of the Study

The study employed the quantitative research method—the justification for selecting the quantitative research method results from the nature of the study. A quantitative research approach follows positivist assumptions and worldviews (Creswell & Creswell, 2017). The quantitative research method uses "measurement and statistics," testable hypotheses, and mathematical modeling to analyze data empirically (Creswell & Creswell, 2017; Easterby-Smith et al., 2018; Hoy & Adams, 2016, p. 1). As the research needs to examine whether the business agility, leanness dimension, and CSR relate to the four dimensions of BSC, a quantitative research method is appropriate. Prior researchers, such as Refera (2020), have conducted a descriptive study on Omo microfinance. However, this study utilizes inferential statistics and correlational tests. Hence, the quantitative approach of the research method is suitable for understanding the relationship between quantifiable variables. Besides, the qualitative research method does not apply to studies encompassing modeling and testing hypotheses (Creswell & Creswell, 2018).

The study examined the relationship between business agility, banking leanness, Corporate Social Responsibility, and the four dimensions of the Balanced Scorecard: financial, customer, business process, and business learning and growth. From research design alternatives, a correlational research design was appropriate because the correlational research design suits studies aimed to test relationships among variables (Cho et al., 2022; Hair & Sarstedt, 2019; Zyphur et al., 2022). The study encompassed a correlational research design, which might help to undertake path analysis further using SEM (Zyphur et al., 2022). The correlational research design was the proper selection as the study encompassed multiple theoretical models and various dimensions explaining latent or unobserved variables explained by one or more variables (Cho et al., 2022; Hair & Sarstedt, 2019). A correlational analysis approach was the research design. The justification for the procedure is that the correlational research design helps to check the statistical association among the proposed variables (Goldberger, 1972).

Research Questions

The study aimed to check the relationship between business agility (BA), lean banking (LB), CSR initiatives, and the four BSC dimensions: finance, customer, business process, and business learning and growth. The problem of operational self-sufficiency might relate to one or more of the examined predictors in the study area (Henock, 2019; Remer & Kattilakoski, 2021). Understanding the direction and strength of the selected variables is vital to proactively take measures and predict the influence of variables under study to prepare for unforeseen financial crises. Therefore, testing the strength and direction of the relationship among the variables would help future researchers and banking industries design predictive models to track the financial and operational trajectory after differentiating the success factors aligned with business sustainability and self-sufficiency. Hence, the study aimed to answer the following two central research questions.

Research Question 1. What is the relationship between business agility (BA), lean banking (LB), CSR initiatives, and the four BSC dimensions?

After checking the existence of a relationship, the following second research question was answered.

Research Question 2. What is the strength and direction of a relationship between business agility (BA), lean banking (LB), CSR initiatives, and the four BSC dimensions?

Hypotheses

Based on the study's sample, statistical inferences can be made about the population following the result of statistical significance and decisions based on the hypothesis testing (Turner et al., 2020). In technical terms, the alternative hypothesis would be tested to the opposite of the alternative hypothesis, which is the null hypothesis. The study employed a correlational research design; the two research questions were answered by testing the stated hypotheses. Future researchers and banking industries may use the results and findings of the correlational analysis. This quantitative study tested the following hypothesized assumptions that accord with the two research questions.

The following correlational hypotheses were tested to answer the first research question.

Null hypothesis: There is no statistically significant correlation between business agility (BA), lean banking (LB), Corporate Social Responsibility (CSR) initiatives, and the four Balanced Scorecard (BSC) dimensions, as measured by Kendall's Tau correlation coefficient (τ) with a small or negligible effect size.

(Null hypothesis: H0: $\tau = 0$, effect size <= small or negligible)

Alternative hypothesis: There is a statistically significant correlation between business agility (BA), lean banking (LB), Corporate Social Responsibility (CSR) initiatives, and the four Balanced Scorecard (BSC) dimensions, as measured by Kendall's Tau correlation coefficient (τ) with a large effect size.

(Alternative hypothesis: Ha: $\tau \neq 0$, the effect size is large)

The following null hypothesis(H0) and alternative (Ha) hypotheses were tested to answer the second research question.

Null hypothesis (H0): The correlation between business agility (BA), lean banking (LB), Corporate Social Responsibility (CSR) initiatives, and the four Balanced Scorecard (BSC) dimensions is not positive and statistically significant, with no or negligible effect size.

(H0: $\tau \leq 0$, the effect size is small or non-existent)

Alternative hypothesis (Ha): The correlation between business agility (BA), lean banking (LB), Corporate Social Responsibility (CSR) initiatives, and the four Balanced Scorecard (BSC) dimensions is positive and significant, with a large effect size.

(H: $\tau > 0$, there is a significantly large effect size).

From the theoretical and empirical standpoint, business agility (BA), lean banking (LB), and CSR initiatives would positively affect the four BSC dimensions. Besides, the four BSC dimensions mediate the relationship between BA, LB, CSR initiatives, and organizational performance (OSS).

Theoretical Framework

Robert Kaplan and David Norton used a new approach in 1992 to measure and assess organizations' performances (Kaplan & Norton, 1992). The BSC approach to measuring performance is employed as a strategic management method. Kaplan and Norton (2007) developed the Balanced Scorecard system. The methodology encompassed four significant dimensions: (1) the customer dimension, (2) the financial dimension, (3) the learning and growth dimension, and (4) the business process dimension. Kaplan and Norton's BSC model helps as a milestone in designing a customized BSC for the banking industry and using significant dimensions as variables or proxy measures of performance in various dimensions. Kaplan's and Norton's (2007) model of BSC is appropriate for this study since the model considered the significant operational and financial performance metrics and indicators of banking industries such as the Ethiopian Omo Bank. Apart from the critical theory of the BSC model of Kaplan and Norton (1992), the study encompasses three other theories to build the theoretical framework. These include David Teece's theory of dynamic capability and strategic management, James Womack and Daniel Jones's theory of lean management, and Howard Bowen's theory of the social responsibility of businesses.

David Teece, Gary Pisano, and Amy Shuen's Theory of Dynamic Capabilities and Strategic Management

Teece et al. (1997) developed the dynamic capability model and framework to win in a competitive market. As a business's main objective is to optimize profitability and get a competitive advantage in changing dynamics, capabilities should be strongly built to meet business agility requirements. The necessary cash flow should be optimized to implement business agility initiatives to improve banking industries' quality and service in technology and other capabilities (Pascale et al., 1997; Teece et al., 1997; Teece, 2017). Hence, according to Teece et al. (1997), wealth creation or organizational success can be realized in an agile business environment by boosting internal capability, which can be explained by cash flow.

James Womack and Daniel Jones's Theory of Lean Management

According to the model introduced by Womack and Jones (1994), organizational performance can be maximized by using a lean management approach and building a lean enterprise. The theory claims that reducing unnecessary steps saves human capital and time. As a result, efficient production can be attained with minimal cost. Building a culture of producing less and avoiding waste would change organizational performance (Womack & Jones, 1994; 1996; 2007). Hence, cost efficiency measured by the cost-to-income ratio can explain the waste and inefficiency of banking share companies.

Howard Bowen and Archie Carroll's Theory of Social Responsibility

The contemporary CSR theory is based on Bowen's (1953) social responsibility theory. Bowen (1953; 2013) claims business enterprises are ethically responsible for community contributions. Based on Bowen's (1953) theory, contemporary scholars such as Carroll (1979; 2021) developed dimensions of corporate social responsibility. Among the dimensions, the economic dimension states that businesses have economic responsibilities. From an organizational standpoint, banking industries are established to give financial opportunities to people experiencing poverty and the most vulnerable part of the community (Ledgerwood, 1998). Banking industries following the examined mission considered women in financial inclusion and opportunities. Such empowerment of women in financial inclusion programs of the banking industry would have a significant contribution not only to the service user of banks but also would have an indirect contribution to the organizational performance (Bhatia & Singh, 2019).

Operational Definitions

Latent Variables: Latent variables cannot be easily observed and measured. However, latent variables represent attributes that can be inferred based on other related observed measures (VandenBos, 2015; Borgstede & Eggert, 2022).

Mediator Variable: The mediator variable is a variable that relates the dependent variable and independent variable (Allen, 2017). An independent variable causes a mediating variable, and the mediating variable influences the dependent variable (Syafiq et al., 2022). Such types of variables are also called intervening variables and are commonly used in path analysis.

Moderator Variable: The moderator variable determines the intensity and direction of a correlation between variables. A moderator variable's value determines an independent variable's effect on the dependent variable (Butler, 2021).

Observed Variable: Observed variables can be any dependent or independent variable that can be measured (Morell & Yang, 2019).

Omo Bank: Omo Bank is a microfinance institution established in Southern Ethiopia in 1996 after a valley and river named Omo (Omo Bank, 2023; UNESCO, 2023).

Panel Data: Panel data is a type of longitudinal dataset that contains values of variables at different time points. Panel datasets combine time series and cross-sectional data and help to analyze controlling individual heterogeneity (Longhi, 2020).

Predictive Analytics: Predictive Analysis is a methodology to estimate the future based on historical data. A predictive model is a model used to estimate the probability of events happening in the future (Siegel, 2020).

Sawla: Sawla is a city in Southern Ethiopia, originally named Felege Neway, founded in 1959 during the period of Haile Selassie (Lindahl, 2008). Sawla District Omo Bank is named after the city of Sawla, the center of the Gofa zone (Omo Bank, 2023).

Structural Equation Modeling (SEM): Structural Equation Modeling is a method of data analysis employed to study the relationship among various variables. Dynamic Structural Equation Modeling (DSEM) is a helpful technique for studying the trend of longitudinal data for many variables at various points in time (Asparouhov et al., 2018).

Assumptions, Limitations, and Delimitations

Researchers must clearly state the study assumptions, limitations, and delimitations. Stating philosophical assumptions paves the way for a reader to understand the foundation of the study from a worldview point (Creswell & Creswell, 2018). The limitation of the study states the downsides of the employed research design. Disclosing the weakness of the design in the limitation section encourages future researchers to test theories employing alternative methodologies (Ross & Zaidi, 2019). For instance, as the research design for the study was a correlation research design, future researchers might conduct quasi-experimental research to check if there are changes due to intervention employing an applied type of research. Delimitation of the study encompasses what is included and excluded from the study (Ferreira, 2018). Readers would generally have a chance to understand the influence of the selected philosophy, research design, and scope on the findings and conclusion.

Assumptions

Every researcher has a philosophical standpoint and preference in selecting the data collection method, data analysis, and interpretation. As Creswell and Creswell (2018) stated, the worldview assumption of the study influences the determination of the examined selection criteria. Contrary to the constructivist and transformative worldview of qualitative research, as the study was quantitative, the study followed a postpositivist approach. The selection of the research method was based on two assumptions—the appropriateness of the selected variables and the dataset's accuracy and reliability. Among the assumptions, the study assumed that the correlational research design was appropriate as the study aimed to identify factors contributing to the success of banking industries, testing the relationship between business agility, lean banking, and the four dimensions of BSC employing longitudinal data (Acock, 2013; Jassim & Abdulwahid, 2021; Kline, 2023; Maryoosh & Hussein, 2022; STATA, 2021; Williams et al., 2018;). As the study employed a purposive sampling approach and reviewed the trend of financial and non-financial dimensions contributing to the ten branches under Sawla District Omo Bank, the study assumes the findings only represent institutions under the study (Andrade, 2021).

Limitations

The limitation of a study is tied to the weakness of the selected research design (Ross & Zaidi, 2019). Consequently, as Ross and Zaidi (2019) stated, the research design influences the findings and conclusions. As the study focused on the microfinance industry in a developing nation, Ethiopia, the study finding was limited to representing the Sawla District Omo Bank. Since the study employed a non-probability sampling, there could be potential inferential statics violations. However, the study employed remedial measures and steps to resolve basic assumptions in the research design. Simultaneously, the study ensured the accuracy of the result to preserve the study's internal validity.

Delimitations

The delimitation of a study is related to the scope and boundary of the study (Ferreira, 2018; Ross & Zaidi, 2019). As the study aimed to analyze the relationship between dimensions of business agility, Corporate Social Responsibility, and the four dimensions of the Balanced Scorecard of Omo Bank, the research findings did not cover un-quantifiable non-financial dimensions of organizational performance. From the timeframe delimitation standpoint, the study only analyzed recent five-year quarterly data trends from 2019-2023. Hence, the findings do not cover the financial trends before 2019. As the study used quantifiable existing financial and non-financial data from Sawla District Omo Bank, only depositors and borrowers of the ten branches were exclusively included. However, from an operational data standpoint, the study does not include non-client residents of the Gofa Zone.

Significance of the Study

Developing nations' microfinance industries face self-sufficiency challenges (Remer & Kattilakoski, 2021). Hence, microfinance managers need to build a system to track the operational and strategic activities of the institution to identify the determining factors leading to low performance and act on multi-dimensional challenges. This study helps the banking industries to understand the relationship between business agility and leanness and CSR initiatives to the four dimensions of BSC (customer, finance, learning and growth, and business process). Understanding the relationship between critical measurement variables eases prediction (Karlan & Luca, 2022)

The study could be used as a source of appropriate performance indicators under each category of BSC dimensions. Besides the traditional key performance indicators in microfinance, micro-credit, and banking industries, there are additional potential indicators in the contemporary business interaction to compete in the digital age and agile money market environment (Yazdi et al., 2022). Identifying additional metrics related to the Balanced Scorecard would significantly expand the theories associated with organizational performance and strategic management in banking industries. Lastly, the suggested extended-comprehensive model of BSC would contribute to managing the institution and activities using a Business Intelligence system and making a data-driven decision. In such applied research, practitioners help shape the real business world (Shapiro, 2020). Apart from contributing to the body of knowledge in business and management, the study would significantly contribute to getting applicable inputs. For instance, input about the failure of performance may inform managers in the area to take proactive measures. For a long-run solution, the study insights may lead to an innovative strategy for improving operational and financial activities (Ode & Ayavoo, 2020).

Transition and Summary

In the chapter 1 foundation of the study, the problem of self-sufficiency in banking industries is defined. The study aimed to identify the relationship between business agility, banking leanness, and initiatives in corporate social responsibility to the four dimensions of the Balanced Scorecard. Moreover, the study helps future researchers eager to develop a predictive model and a comprehensive and customized Balanced Scorecard for Banking industries such as microfinance, micro-credit, and banking institutions. The public data of the Microfinance Information Exchange data shows a challenge to the self-sufficiency of microfinance. Prior researchers have tried to identify the financial, customer, growth and learning, and business process dimensions of a

Balanced Scorecard as the main determining factors of self-sufficiency. However, this study mainly focused on whether business agility, banking leanness, and Corporate Social Responsibility initiatives contributed to the industry's self-sufficiency and competitiveness. Chapter 2 states the review of literature on Balanced Scorecards and approaches in measuring various dimensions. Chapter 3 presents the research design, research method, sampling technique, data collection, and method of data analysis.

Chapter 2: Review of the Professional and Academic Literature

Literature Search Strategy

The literature search strategy section is relevant to inform the reader about the literature content, the organization of the review, and the primary search strategy and evaluate how the utilized articles are current and peer-reviewed. From ethical standards of literature review analysis and synthesis, the openness of a researcher paves the way for future researchers to identify gaps and work on areas of improvement in the existing literature and potential strategies. Besides, the literature search strategy section helps to objectively evaluate the quality, validity, and credibility of the literature included (Kuo, 2022).

Content of The Literature

The study aimed to identify the relationship between a balanced scorecard's four dimensions with metrics related to CSR, Business Agility, and Leanness. Prior researchers have tried to identify the relationship between the four dimensions of a Balanced Scorecard: financial dimension, customer dimension, learning and growth dimension, and business process dimension. Initially, literature on the topic of the Balanced Scorecard is identified. Creswell and Creswell's (2018) and Machi and McEvoy's (2022) suggested approaches are followed to determine the content of the literature. Based on the reviewer's research interest in financial industries, the subject matter included in the literature focuses studies mainly on microfinance, micro-credit, and banks.

The review was undertaken to identify research gaps in the previously published academic literature. Based on the search result, quantitative studies were conducted on

BSC in most developed nations, not in developing nations of Sub-Saharan Africa like Ethiopia. As the performance management system is at an infant stage of adoption and implementation in developing countries, there are few quantitative studies in regions of East Africa under the topic of a Balanced Scorecard (Refera, 2020). Refera's (2020) analysis relies on a qualitative, not quantitative, approach from the identified recent publications. Besides, prior scholars might have difficulty collecting data for research due to the absence of database management and a real-time data reporting system. Similarly, few studies are identifying the relationship between Corporate Social Responsibility, Business Agility, and Leanness and the four dimensions of the Balanced Scorecard. Hence, the literature search topic was confined to the search for proxy measures of the respective significant variables of Corporate Social Responsibility, Business Agility, and Leanness.

The study was expected to fill the research gap by analyzing the problem of self-sufficiency and identifying factors related to CSR, Business Agility, and leanness. Hence, the study would significantly contribute to the existing literature since it encompasses a new region with comprehensive BSC dimensions and a timely topic (Creswell & Creswell, 2018). Due to the reviewer's research interest and the existence of relevant prior quantitative research findings, the significant areas reviewed include topics on adoption challenges to BSC, predictors of performance, developing customized BSC, and an approach to comparing and ranking banks based on BSC. Besides, related literature and original theories associated with metrics of BSC, business agility, and leanness are defined and analyzed. Essential variables related to the main theories of Balanced Scorecard, Corporate Social Responsibility, Business Agility, and Leanness, their respective explanatory (independent) variables, and their potential relationship with business sustainability and organizational performance are identified and defined. As commonly undertaken in quantitative research, claims were analyzed to check the coincidence of findings with original theories related to organizational performance and strategic management in banking industries. The primary literature source includes databases of ProQuest, JSTOR, Google Scholar, Harvard Business Review magazine publications, and scholarly books.

The Organization of The Review

Following Creswell and Creswell's (2018) approach, the literature was organized in two ways after identifying related literature. First, recent literature on the topic of the Balanced Scorecard was identified. Assembling the subject area based on the five major issues: Balanced Scorecard, Corporate Social Responsibility, Business Agility, and Business Leanness helps identify research gaps. Simultaneously, such an approach contributes to the existing literature on the themes (Creswell & Creswell, 2018). The objective of identifying BSC-related articles was to check the evolution of BSC and recent findings on the relationship between the four dimensions of BSC. Second, as previous studies rarely studied the relationship of BSC's four dimensions in conjunction with CSR, business agility, and leanness proxy variables, the main theories and claims concerning business sustainability and organizational performance are analyzed.

The Strategy for Searching the Literature

Based on Creswell and Creswell's (2018) recommended search strategy, topics related to Balanced Scorecards, Corporate Social Responsibility, Business Agility, and Business Leanness are searched. As the proposed research question for the study relies on identifying relationships among variables, most of the articles and definitions coincide with quantitative literature. Simultaneously, while searching previous literature reviews, as the study focused on financial industries such as banks, microfinance, and micro-credit, the three keywords limit the search and identify banking industry-focused articles solely.

To narrow the search in databases of ProQuest, JSTOR, Google Scholar, Harvard Business Review magazine publications, and scholarly books, from the subject area dimension, critical terms used include organizational performance, strategic performance, data analysis, financial analysis, financial intelligence, enterprise resource planning system, information technology, agile leadership, business agility, agile banking, lean leadership, bank, banking, microfinance, microcredit, balanced scorecard, BSC, social responsibility performance, performance management, financial, customer satisfaction, business process, learning, and growth, correlation, relationship, return on asset, financial inclusion, employee turnover, cash flow, cost efficiency, operational efficiency, self-sufficient, sustainability, prediction, Structural Equation Modeling, and SEM. The databases' advanced search feature has helped the reviewer to filter and find articles based on combined keywords, recent publications, and the study scope. The search strategy helped the reviewer to collect and assemble only relevant literature (Machi & McEvoy, 2022).

Peer-Reviewed Sources and Current References

According to the American Psychological Association (2020), peer-reviewed sources are considered quality papers in the scientific and academic community. Besides getting quality papers, peer-reviewed literature sources are deemed credible and valid

(Kuo, 2022). As peer-reviewed publications go the step of review as per ethical standards of research, the reviewer has utilized an advanced search feature for filtering peer-reviewed literature. In addition, using recent literature is recommended by the scientific community. The American Psychological Association (2020) recommends also using previous works directly linked to original theories. Consequently, the reviewer has included original theoretical articles from the 1990s to inform a reader about the foundational concepts related to critical variables and metrics.

To write the literature review of doctoral study, peer-reviewed articles, scholarly books, textbooks, and government, academic, and scholarly websites are used. Of the 233 references, 174 are peer-reviewed articles, comprising 75 percent of the total references. Among the selected peer-reviewed articles, 87 percent (150) were published within five years. The reviewer chose the remaining 24 articles (13 percent of the peer-reviewed articles) to inform a reader about the theoretical foundation of major themes assessed in the literature review published in 2017 and before. 39 scholarly books and popular textbooks, about 64 percent of references used in the literature, are from the recent five-year publication. The Harvard Business Press mainly publishes the books used for the literature review. The remaining 36 percent of books used are aligned with the original theories of concepts used in the literature. Besides, 17 references were used from recent government, scholarly websites, and articles from organizations and research institutes. Details about the breakdown of references are indicated in Table 1.

Table 1.

Audit of References

No.	Source of references	2017 and earlier		2018 up to 2023		Total sources	
		number	percentage	number	percentage	number	percentage
1	Peer-reviewed articles	24	13%	150	87%	174	75%
2	Scholarly books and textbooks	14	36%	25	64%	39	17%
3	Government, academic, and scholarly websites	3	19%	17	81%	20	8%
Total sources		41	18%	192	82%	233	100%

Balanced Scorecard

In 1992, Kaplan and Norton (2007) first developed the BSC as a strategic

management approach to measure and evaluate organizational performance. The scholars

included financial and non-financial metrics with four broad categories. These include the

customer, internal, business process, learning and growth, and financial dimensions. In

this approach, Kaplan and Norton aimed to design the BSC tool to track the daily routine

operational activities per the long-run strategic goal of companies. Furthermore, Kaplan

and Norton (2007) suggest four significant steps to prepare BSC dimensions that fit the

company's purpose. These include defining a vision for individual dimensions,

communicating and integrating activities to strategic goals, planning projects and activities that coincide with the strategic plan, and customizing the metrics through learning and gathering opinions.

Recent studies on the BSC application in the banking industry focused on four primary areas. First, some studies focus on the challenge in business sectors to adopt BSC as their performance measurement, and others tried to encompass the BSC system of strategic measurement customizing to their scenario (Al-Alawi, 2018; Al-Hawatmeh, 2021; Chiang et al., 2020; Singh & Simple, 2018; Zhou et al., 2020). For instance, Singh and Simple (2018) empirically assessed the factors affecting the adoption of BSC as a performance management system. They found that employees' behavior and the potential of the organization matter. Besides, Singh & Simple (2018) contend that managerial bodies' willingness and proper communication pave the way to introduce the system.

In this digital age, we need to customize our Key Performance Indicators (KPIs) following the time and change in variables to have a unique contemporary picture of an organization's performance. That seems to be why Al-Alawi (2018) developed a "strategic model map" for the online banking system in Bahrain, considering the BSC approach. However, this study only focused on theoretical development. Moreover, it does not show an empirical aspect. On the other end, some financial institutions use the BSC approach to determine the decision-making areas of a particular project. For example, a recent study shows that financial sectors used the BSC tool to measure loss and inefficiencies in investment projects (Zhou et al.,2020). Therefore, Zhou and his friends recommend that technological and financial adequacy determine the decision on credit limits by the public, private, and foreign banks.

As the nature of the institution changes, metrics must be changed under each dimension of BSC. For instance, financial sectors that establish alliances, such as marketing alliances, develop a customized dimension of performance that bridges the goal of the service and banking industry (Chiang et al.,2020). These metrics included the cooperative alliance aspect as an additional dimension to the BSC, with thirty indicators under five significant dimensions. Hence, different banking industries introduced the BSC system and checked its applicability in the industry (Al-Hawatmeh, 2021).

The second area of recent literature under BSC focused on identifying the significant predictor of performance in their industry (Al-Busaidi & Al-Muharrami, 2021; Nhung & Anh, 2019; Owusu, 2017; Taamneh et al., 2018; Zahoor & Sahaf, 2018). The success factor for organizations within the same industry may not be the same for all financial sectors. For instance, Owusu (2017) revealed that introducing a Business Intelligence System (BIS) in the banking industry would positively affect learning and growth, internal processes, and customer dimensions. Such findings further consider BIS technology with a BSC system for dual benefit. The other recent study by Zahoor and Sahaf (2018) shows that every four dimensions have a positive causal link. This study indicated that the BSC dimensions of customers, internal and business processes, learning and growth, and financial dimensions directly impact banks' performance.

Apart from the interrelationship among BSC dimensions, recent studies revealed mediating factors between the BSC dimensions and the performance of organizations. For instance, when we consider the 1988 Organ's theory of Organizational Citizenship Behavior (OCB) as a proxy of Human Resource Management (HRM), it has a positive mediating effect on the performance of the business under this study (Taamneh et al.,

2018). Note here that there are peculiar studies that are different from BSC to check and balance the performance of financial industries using different approaches like financial ratios and KPIs. For example, Nhung and Anh (2019) considered the impact of mergers and acquisitions on banking efficiency and performance in Vietnam. Furthermore, the study uncovered that M&A positively contributes to return on assets. Besides, Al-Busaidi & Al-Muharrami (2021) identified a significant positive contribution of Information Communication Technology (ICT) in the three BSC dimensions (customer, internal business process, and learning and growth).

The third aspect in which recent literature focuses was on developing theories and variables beyond BSC as an extended metric to measure the performance of financial industries and select strategic target areas for decision-making. For instance, Bazrkar and Iranzadeh (2017) used the BSC approach to establish a strategic process to implement the Lean Six Sigma methodology. Combining the two approaches, the scholars suggest managers focus on choosing the strategic process among alternatives for the strategic area of work instead of working on weaknesses. Likewise, some further studies link BSC and Lean Six Sigma approaches to developing a new quality model to improve organizational performance and customer satisfaction (Bazrkar et al., 2018). Mohammad and Omidi (2017) considered a combination of BSC and CSR as performance evaluation and decision-making criteria. Based on their study, return on investment, debt ratio, and lower energy consumption are essential strategic areas to focus on in the banking industry.

Similarly, scholars also used extended BSC with a cross-efficiency approach to select a strategic process (Bazrkar et al., 2018). Their study found that employee satisfaction, the environment, and communication attributes in society determine the rank of the strategic process using the Six Sigma approach to "reduce weaknesses and increase profitability, employee satisfaction, quality of product and customer satisfaction." As the previous scholars mentioned above, Akman and Turan (2021) further developed an integrated approach as an extension of BSC, including risk and agile dimensions. They contend that it is vital to consider different types of risk (operational, strategic, and external) and agile dimensions to compete in the digital era. Their approach could help to see views beyond BSC.

The fourth and final area of literature in BSC focuses on comparing and ranking banking industries based on the four BSC dimensions. For instance, Pradhan and Murari (2019) used the BS approach to compare two banks in Bhutan. They found that one of the bank's internal business process dimensions is weak compared to the other. Employing the BSC approach and Multicriteria Decision Making (MCDM) method, a recent study ranked and assessed the performance of banks under investigation (Amir et al.,2020).

From the article reviewed above, readers can understand how recent scholars have tried to extend the four dimensions of BSC, encompassing other relevant dimensions in the banking industry. Regarding the Microfinance industry, there needs to be more research in developing dimensions and metrics with the BSC dimensions (Refera, 2020). Hence, this calls for further study in developing a timely, comprehensive, Balanced Scorecard tool for microfinance institutions in emerging economies. For simplicity and to draw a conceptual and theoretical framework for the proposed study, the study tested the relationship between each respective proxy variable of business agility, lean banking, and CSR with the four dimensions of the Balanced Scorecard.

Agile And Lean Leadership

In this digital era, business industries and their respective managers must adapt to changes to ensure the possible implementation of new practices to boost performance (Kenny, 2020). Implementing the Business Analytics Initiative and agile approach to executing activities has a significant role in microbusiness (Peeters et al., 2022; Piot-Lepetit & Nzongang, 2021). In Piot-Lepetit and Nzongang's (2021) study on Cameroon Bank, the finding attested to the possible implementation of Business Analytics to help managers in the data-driven decision-making process. However, the contextual situation determines the deployment of a data analytics initiative. Besides, business agility and leanness would likely improve operational speed and team commitment (Peeters et al., 2022). Different studies on the agile dimension look at agile predictors as a mediator, while others consider it the fifth dimension of the Balanced scorecard.

Corporate Social Responsibility

The reputation of firms influences customer attraction. In developed nations, financial industries care much for their brand and name and participate in corporate social responsibility practices; this, in turn, leads to being registered as a reputable firm and being competitive in the market (Scott et al., 2019). Allet (2017) identified legal and infrastructural constraints to incorporating social responsibility as an indirect target to strengthen the organization's sustainability. There needs to be more practice and research studied on Microfinance in this regard.

Literature Review on Key Concepts and Variables

High Performance, Organizational Success, and Sustainability

Organizational performance, success, and financial sustainability are interconnected strategic areas for financial and banking industries. Business and management scholars link organizational performance with two main areas: employees meeting corporate targets and working process improvement (Harvard Business Review, 2017). From the banking industry's point of view, organizational performance may relate to achievements in metrics of profitability, customer satisfaction, reduced cost of operation, and reduced risk. Each variable mentioned has a cause-and-effect relationship.

As a financial institution, risks are prevalent in various forms (Harvard Business Review, 2017). Banking industries would have credit risk, which aligns with borrowers' failure to meet financial obligations due to different ups and downs of the market operation or business. When borrowers have multidimensional opportunities to make money and grow, the likelihood of loan repayment increases, leading to a reduced risk. If such experiences continue with taking calculated risks, banking industries such as microfinance would have a greater chance of sustainability due to success in achieving reduced risk.

The other dimension is achieving higher performance with the least cost principle (Harvard Business Review, 2020). There are various measures of profitability. As the number of clients increases and when employees are required to execute operational and financial activities increases, the administrative cost may significantly influence the institution's profitability. For instance, if the interest earned from a loan has an insignificant contribution to the rate of return, the financial welfare of the institution would be severely affected. As corporate financial institutions do not solely focus on revenue and cost in the contemporary era, the shareholder equity of institutions also determines the sector's sustainability. Financial organizations also have a minimum threshold of financial obligation, which central and national banks request. In case of inability to meet the liquidity, banking industries may lose recognition. The financial and non-financial aspects related to customer satisfaction need to be optimized to ensure the sustainability and competitiveness of the industry and to continue as a reputable and sustainable financial organization. Institutions should adequately manage strategic initiatives to achieve the targeted strategic goal, and organizations can succeed in action (Harvard Business Review, 2020).

Success requires a consistent commitment to achieving strategic objectives and activities. Apart from maximizing profitability, shareholder value, customer satisfaction, and minimizing risk, financial industries' adoption of innovative ideas and technology is crucial. Simultaneously, employees are engines to execute strategic areas, so employee satisfaction should not be left behind. Corporate organizations pay attention to hiring talented employees to boost organizational performance. Recent literature regarding success reveals various approaches to the pathway to success. Graban and Wheeler (2019) suggest double-checking whether organizations achieve the planned targets. Due to various internal and external factors, organizational performance may increase or decrease year-to-year or quarterly. Graban and Wheeler (2019) noted that unless financial sectors consistently achieve targets, occasional triumph in financial and non-financial metrics would not result in success. The other area of concern is the predictability of the future. Successful organizations can predict the future and work on improvement areas to enhance institutions' competitive capacity in regional, national, continental, and global markets. Hence, Graban and Wheeler (2019) recommend diligently checking approaches and areas of improvement for successful organizational achievement.

The sustainability of financial industries such as microfinance depends on performance and achievement in various dimensions. Most of the earliest research on the sustainability of banking industries aligns solely with financial dimensions. However, recent studies have expanded the dimensions by adding environmental, social, and governance (ESG) aspects (García-Pérez et al., 2017). The ecological dimension encompasses the participation of financial sectors in funding and participating in environmental initiatives such as energy, carbon emission, and environmental management.

Concurrently, financial industries started to contribute to the social welfare of marginalized communities through economic participation by giving loan opportunities to the vulnerable and assisting initiatives in labor, human rights, and community participation (García-Pérez et al., 2017). The governance dimension relates to the practice of banking industries in re-structuring the organization and implementing vital leadership approaches proven to result in sustainable growth and development. In the digital era, financial sectors compete and outstate sustainability metrics of the ESG dimensions from other competitors by optimizing internal organizational performance, contributing to the community, and participating in global initiatives and leadership (García-Pérez et al., 2017). A recent study on rural microfinance reveals that strong leadership positively contributes to the sustainability of microfinance (Rambu Atahau et al., 2020).

Success Metrics and Dimensions of Organizational Performance of Banking

There are many measures of the success of financial organizations. However, traditionally, scholars have studied various quantitative studies on the role of financial metrics in assuring the success and sustainability of financial sectors such as micro-credit and microfinance institutions. The transition of microfinance from microfinance to bank initiated scholars to study sustainability and success factors (García-Pérez et al., 2017). According to Kumar et al. (2021), peer-reviewed articles from accounting and management journals comprised one hundred fourteen studies. The scholars found various critics of using Kaplan and Norton's (1992) approach to measuring organizational performance based on the BSC four dimensions. The critics align with either contending BSC to be used as a performance measurement or management control system. However, Kumar et al. (2021) revealed that most scholars still accept the contribution of the Balanced Scorecard approach for measuring organizational performance. Simultaneously, the scholars identified that the regression model is commonly used to check the cause and effect of metrics included in the customer, internal business, growth and learning, and financial dimension of BSC. A recent study also supports the BSC approach's relevance in measuring the banking industry's profitability, sustainability, and competitiveness (Gupta et al., 2020). However, Kaplan and Norton's (1992) BSC dimensions and previous studies do not holistically encompass relevant dimensions such as CSR metrics, Agile leadership, and Lean leadership dimensions. Hence, eight extensive BSC variables and metrics measurements are defined and explained in the following review literature section.

Financial Metrics

Financial dimensions are the typical traditional approach to measuring organizational performance in the banking sector. This section discusses the meaning and approach to measuring the identified financial dimensions by reviewing relevant literature. Kaplan and McMillan (2021) argue that the Balanced Scorecard approach to measuring organizational performance was adopted for two main reasons. First, to avoid the limitation of the traditional approach solely focused on measuring financial dimensions. Hence, the Balanced Scorecard approach was believed to encompass non-financial performance dimensions. Second, employing a strategy map in the Balanced Scorecard approach helped visualize how financial institutions' multidimensional strategic targets are interlinked. In the Environment, Social, and Governance era, financial dimensions are relevant to ensuring the sustainability of banking industries. Weber's (2017) recent findings support the stated claim. In the research analysis of Chinese banks, Weber found ''a bi-directional causality between financial performance and sustainability'' (Weber, 2017, p. 358).

Various financial and business management scholars have utilized returns, ratios, and other relevant profitability and shareholder-value maximization performance metrics. The frequently used metrics to show the level of financial performance vary from nation to nation. According to Refera's (2020) review of literature analysis, there are five significant financial metrics associated with Ethiopian microfinance. These include ''adjusted return on asset, adjusted return on equity, operating self-sufficiency, portfolio at risk > 30 days and the ratio of operating expense to loan portfolio'' (Refera, 2020, p. 173).

Return on Asset (ROA)

Based on Frisch's (2014) basic definition, return on asset is the proportion of net income to total assets. The balance sheet is used for the financial analysis as a source for the total asset amount. The measure of return on asset informs analysts about the efficiency of the asset to create profitability. In financial intelligence, return on assets tells the percentage of every invested currency unit, which results in profitability (Berman et al., 2013). In providing various financial and operational services, financial sectors such as micro-credit, microfinance, and share company banks invest in assets such as machinery equipment, transportation automobiles, and various plants. Hence, return on asset informs how effective is the financial sector in utilizing the assets to make a profit. The rate of change in return on assets tells the improvement or reduction of efficiency of using assets to generate income. Moreover, higher ratios are preferred. Simultaneously, such metrics are valuable for comparing the relative differences between banking industries in achieving efficiency in utilizing assets for a better return (Berman et al., 2013; Frisch, 2014).

Return on Equity (ROE)

As the name indicates, Return on Equity (ROE) is computed by dividing net income by owners' equity (Frisch, 2014). The ROE is the percentage of a generated return due to an investment held by the institution's owner. Equity refers to the net worth, while asset indicates the company's ownership (Berman et al., 2013). Hence, ROE is a vital measure to check how the institution is getting a return from investment in treasury bonds. The ROE measure does not consider risk in the computation. Like the ROA measure, the financial ratio metric of ROE is helpful to compare the relative difference among banks and to check the growth rate to understand annual or quarterly improvement in getting a higher or reduced profit from shareholders' equity (Berman et al., 2013; Frisch, 2014).

Operating Self-Sufficiency (OSS)

Operating self-sufficiency is a commonly used ratio in the financial analysis of microfinance (Ledgerwood, 1998). Traditionally, OSS is used as a metric to check and balance the strengths and weaknesses of financial industries in developing nations and as a measure of sustainability. Operating self-sufficiency is the ratio of financial income to financial and operating cost and loan loss provision. Alternatively, OSS can be calculated by dividing the total operating income by operating expenses. As the name indicates, the OSS evaluates the capacity of a bank to operate using income and not requiring funds from other sources. The higher the ratio, the larger the institution's ability and the less dependency on external finance (Ledgerwood, 1998).

Portfolio at Risk (PAR) (> 30 days)

A portfolio at risk is the ratio of the loan balance in arrears to the outstanding value of the loan (Ledgerwood, 1998). The PAR measures the total balance in arrears and the due loan balance. The portfolio at risk checks the quality of the portfolio based on the aging analyses of the loans. In microfinance terms, a portfolio at risk indicates the likelihood of loan losses. In comparison, while the ROA and ROE measure the return or profit generated due to either assets or investment in equity, PAR checks the risk of loans disbursed to clients (Ledgerwood, 1998).

The Ratio of Operating Expense to Loan Portfolio (OE/LP)

As the name indicates, OE/LP is calculated by dividing the operating expense by the loan portfolio. The OE-LP measure tells the percentage of the bank's operating expense spent for loan portfolio coverage. The OE-LP metric informs the efficiency of a bank in managing expenses. Simultaneously, the measurement tells the institution's capacity to generate income from a loan portfolio covering expenses (Refera, 2020).

Customer Dimension Metrics

Customer satisfaction based on customer experience drives customer loyalty and customer retention. According to Kaplan and McMillan (2021), a customer can be any stakeholder who benefits from the operation of financial services in the case of banking industries. Kaplan and McMillan (2021) believe in a positive return from a satisfied and profitable customer. The stated scholars argue that as the clients are happy with the service and product of an institution, the likelihood of customer loyalty and retention would be boosted. Simultaneously, in the case of microfinance and financial sectors, if clients earn additional profit from the loan service, customers' profitability, in turn, calls back to the industry to establish a strong tie and loyalty with the company.

In the case of the ESG era, quality of service and processing time determine the creation of satisfied and profitable customers. As Williams (2018) states, although the Balanced Scorecard approach of Kaplan and Norton (1992) has drawbacks in measuring customer satisfaction with a weighted scorecard, the system links how the four dimensions of BSC are interrelated. The strategic question from the customer dimension of BSC is to identify how customers see the provider or the business. According to Kaplan and Norton's (1992) viewpoint, to make the targeted profitability, companies need to identify clear goals from the customer's dimension and state the unit of measurement to the set objectives.

Customer Satisfaction Using the Likert Scale

Researchers and analysts can measure customer dimensions from various approaches. Huang et al. (2018) contend that businesses should go beyond the target of customer service by turning angry customers by designing alternative methods to create loyal customers. As a strategy, Huang et al. (2018) suggest three main approaches: surprising customers by responding timely, solving the problems of an unhappy customer, and creating value for a business through positive gestures. Traditionally, such customer experience dimensions are measured using a Likert scale. Alternatively, the timeliness of service delivery can be measured by business researchers by putting a range of minutes, for example, as service delivered in sixty minutes or more, twenty-one minutes to fifty-nine minutes, six minutes to twenty minutes, and five minutes or less (Huang et al., 2018).

In recent literature, the approach to measuring customer satisfaction is diverse, depending on the type of business and the strategic objective of the sector. For instance, Reichheld and Dunlop (2022) recommend asking four questions related to humanity, transparency, capability, and reliability of the service delivery. Reichheld and Dunlop (2022) follow the Likert scale approach that Huang et al. (2018) used to measure customer satisfaction. The difference relies on the area of attention in customer dimensions. Hence, Reichheld and Dunlop (2022) used to score the customer who rated the service as positive, neutral, and hostile. If the survey method is employed in research studies measuring customer experience, the approaches would have better precision.

Huang et al. (2018) and Reichheld and Dunlop's (2022) approach to measuring customer dimension relies on Refera's (2020) dimension to measuring customer satisfaction.

Customer Retention Using Percentage Change

Due to technological adoption and economic constraints, developing nations have yet to adopt a research-based method of evaluating customer satisfaction; instead, it is measured using the percentage change in the number of customers in various groups of services. In the micro-credit, microfinance, and banking industries of developing nations such as Africa, the rate of change of the number of depositors and loanees is a commonly used approach to checking the organizational performance in the customer dimension (Refera, 2020). Hence, this study used a quantitative approach to measuring the relationship by using the number of loanees and the number of voluntary depositors. Consequently, the study checked how the percentage change in the number of clients in the two services (saving and loan) relates to the industry's profitability, sustainability, and competitiveness.

Internal Business Process Dimension Metrics

The internal business process dimension of Kaplan and Norton (1992) relies on improving the process of activities under an organization. As the business process improves, the adopted approach would likely boost efficiency in cost management and the industry's overall financial and operational activities. When the internal business process is enhanced, institutions can ease capital, asset, and plant property management by introducing a scientifically proven and advanced approach to undertaking routine and strategic activities. Resource management coincides with cost management (Kaplan & Norton, 1992).

The main objective under the internal business process dimension is to identify areas of improvement and work on a strategy to excel rivals or competitors in a similar industry in the national or international market. Various sectors use multiple approaches to improve the internal process. The method varies from industry to industry. In the case of banking industries, using cycle time (duration of loan application processing) and borrowers per loan officer can be used to check the performance of microfinance businesses (Refera, 2020).

Cycle Time: Duration of Loan Application Processing

The internal business process should drive customer satisfaction. Kaplan and Norton's (1992) claim indicates how each dimension is interlinked and contributes to the overall performance of a corporation. For instance, with the introduction of an improved business system, the cycle time in a process taken from start to finish would decrease. A decrease in cycle time would increase customer satisfaction. Refera's (2020) review of articles related to the microfinance industry indicates a cycle time that shows the duration of loan application processing as a significant metric to measure a change in the process of banking businesses. From the customers' point of view, as the wait time for the request and approval of a given activity increases, the process would disappoint customers and lead to reduced loyalty to the industry. Adopting an improved system to reduce the cycle depends on an institution's financial status (Kaplan & Norton, 1992; Refera, 2020). In the case of developed nations, introducing an automated system to facilitate the business process is relatively more accessible compared to banking industries in developing countries.

Borrowers Per Loan Officers: Proxy of Operational Efficiency

Out of the operational activities of microfinance, loans and saving services are among the most common in developing countries. Ali et al. (2020) state the relevance of borrowers per staff as the proxy for financial and operational efficiency. The number of borrowers per loan officer informs the workload of a given loan officer handling cases related to disbursement or loaning service. As the value of borrowers per loan officer is high, such experience in the industry indicates the productivity of officers handling more cases. The reverse is valid for a lower ratio of borrowers per loan officer. Institutions can achieve such expected operational efficiency by increasing employees' productivity (Ali et al., 2020).

The approach to increasing employees' productivity depends on the level of growth and development of the nation in which the corporate business resides. Looking at the recent arguments, for instance, Teevan (2021) claims that the work setting is changing to a hybrid form in which some workers work from an office, and others use virtual interaction. Hence, working on the well-being of employees is recommended. As the well-being of employees is protected, employees are likely to be more productive in operational activities. Besides, in the case of teamwork requirements, as employees collaborate, employees would be effective in undertaking the required task (Teevan, 2021).

On the contrary, Markovitz (2022) focuses mainly on the system, not the employees, to achieve a productive performance. According to Markovitz's (2022) point of view, organizations should build and establish a system to resolve client cases. Creating a system would enhance the capability of workers to collaborate and work on achieving the organizational goal by simplifying communication and decision-making processes through the system. Stoddard's (2022) claim coincides with Markovitz's (2022) argument. For better productivity of employees, business organizations need to adopt tools and systems to enhance employee productivity. For instance, innovative and technologically assisted tools would likely ease the hassle for employees and clients, resulting in productive work and efficiency for faster loans and saving transactions (Markovitz, 2022; Stoddard, 2022).

In addition to the cycle time and loan per loan officer, according to Refera (2020), microfinance industries can achieve improved business processes by having a scientifically proven strategy to implement plans and working on the research and development aspect of the industry. Vermeulen (2017) stated that some scholars need help differentiating strategies from plans. Accordingly, business sectors with alternative implementation strategies reduce the chance of organizational performance failure. Investing in research and development has a significant effect on business processes. There are controversies in this regard, mentioning that a mere investment without explorative research findings may not boost the competitive capability of the business (Nagle & Teodoridis, 2020).

Learning and Growth Dimension Metrics

The learning and growth dimension aligns with organizational performance-determining factors such as technology and human capital. In the traditional approach of measuring performance using a Balanced Scorecard, Kaplan and Norton (2007) attest that the main objective of the dimension is to introduce a system of change and improvement to achieve organizational short-run and long-run targets. With the broad aim of introducing change and improved technological adoption and implementation, corporate industries can work on the goal of technology leadership and learning (Kaplan & Norton, 2007).

In the contemporary era, Kaplan and McMillan (2021) combined the technology dimension of the learning and growth dimension with the previous internal business process dimension. Though the internal business process relates significantly to the learning and growth dimensions, looking at each is vital. For instance, in the case of internal business processes, one of the standard metrics used to evaluate the extent is cycle time. To optimize customer satisfaction, a reduced cycle time of operational activities attracts customers and increases sales in the product market. In the money market of the banking industry, such as microfinance, reduced cycle time increases the likelihood of customers willing to borrow money to invest and get a return on investment. Technology adoption and improved human resource skills are required for such a prevalence of reduced cycle time (Kaplan & McMillan, 2021).

From Refera's (2020) suggested metrics of learning and growth dimension in Ethiopian microfinance, there are four significant areas of attention. These include employee satisfaction, training, and performance evaluation of employees from the human resource dimension, investment in information systems and information technology, and innovation from the technology aspect. The reader should note that the internal business process and the learning and growth dimensions are intertwined in a cause-and-effect relationship.

Employee Satisfaction: Employee Turnover Rate

Employee satisfaction is equally crucial as customer satisfaction. Chamberlain and Zhao (2019) state that a happy employee drives customer satisfaction. Chamberlain and Zhao (2019) claim a robust statistical relationship between employee and customer satisfaction. As the well-being of employees is protected, employees would likely be happy and be triggered to help the customers of a corporation. The well-being programs may encompass employees' physical, mental, emotional, and other multidimensional aspects to boost workplace satisfaction. As a proxy measure of employee satisfaction, Kenny (2021) states some relevant key performance indicators.

Among the identified metrics, the lost time injury frequency rate (LTIFR) measures the frequency of injuries in a given time interval. Alternatively, accident reports and hazard reports have a negative relationship with employee satisfaction. Employee turnover is another proxy measure of employee satisfaction. Traditionally, a reduced employee turnover is a good indicator of employee satisfaction. Gautier et al. (2022) coincide employee turnover with employee longevity. As employee turnover increases, employee longevity decreases. The reverse is true when employee turnover is reduced. However, on some occasions, though an employee is satisfied with the work environment and other benefits, social and other factors may affect the turnover rate of employees in a corporation. Gautier et al. (2022) use full-time employee status and internal rotation to maximize employee satisfaction. Technically, the employee turnover rate is the ratio of the total number of employees who left the company to the current employees working actively in the institution. The turnover rate is expressed in percentages (Gautier et al., 2022).

Investment in Information Systems and Information Technology

Investing in a corporation's information systems and technology is critical to improving business processes. Accordingly, such a coincidence implies how the two dimensions of a balanced scorecard are interrelated. As a result, Kaplan and McMillan (2021) combined the two dimensions named process and technology dimensions. Based on the definition, the learning and growth dimension is the basis for improvement in the business process dimension. Hence, a significant amount of finance may be required for system implementation for business process improvement and improved adoption and implementation of enhanced business intelligence processes.

More than 81% of banks, according to Jordan-Smith's (2022) analysis, are willing to invest a significant amount of money in modernizing the banking system. There are various reasons behind the claim and optimism toward the investment in information technology and techniques. For instance, investment in technology would likely reduce threats from rival banks. Besides, investment in technology is indispensable due to the emerging demand of customers to get a virtual and online service and the customers' need for improved cycle time (Jordan-Smith, 2022). For this study, investment in the internal banking system can be traced from the expenditure for adopting and implementing the system.

Corporate Social Responsibility (CSR) Dimensions and Corporate Social Performance (CSP) Metrics

The CSR initiatives' definition and objective are seen in various ways from different paradigms of thought. According to Carroll (2021), there are two evolutionary thoughts regarding the theories of CSR. The first period encompasses the year 1950 up to

1999. The second is from 2000 to 2020. Carroll (2021) claims that the advocacy of CSR was started by Bowen (1953). To understand the traditional definition of CSR, analyzing Bowen's (1953) definition is a foundation for the theories of CSR and Corporate Social Performance (CSP) (Carroll, 2018; 2021).

According to Bowen's (1953) point of view, businesses must be responsible for the communities. The expected responsibility is associated with managing the business and contributing to society. In 1979, Carroll (2021) developed four dimensions of CSR to measure the performance aspect. These include corporate industries' discretionary, ethical, legal, and economic responsibilities. The discretionary responsibilities are voluntary-based responsibilities of businesses in philanthropic areas. Companies may contribute as philanthropists by donating funds and volunteering by investing hours and relevant resources for social welfare. Ethically, more than legal responsibilities, society expects businesses to act in ethical ways. Legally, companies must go hand in hand with the rules and regulations of business standards in a given nation. The economic responsibility of a company is to produce goods and services. Accordingly, the four types of duties can be applied in the consumer market, environmental areas, solving discriminatory practices, and product and occupational safety (Carroll, 2021).

From 2000 to 2020, scholars further identified areas of business responsibilities by answering the question of to whom businesses are responsible, in which areas, and the ethical grounds for executing the duties as a business (Carroll, 2021). In general, the 1990s articles and analysis focus on defining CSR and broadening the concepts related to the social responsibility theory. However, in the 2000s, the period is notified by scholarly articles identifying the significant relationship between social performance and financial performance. In this regard, literature has shown a meaningful positive relationship between CSR dimensions in CSP and financial metrics in a corporate industry (Carroll, 2021).

In the case of microfinance-based research on the relationship between CSR and operational self-sufficiency, Hussain et al. (2020) found a significant mediating impact of CSR on the autonomy of banking industries. According to Hussain et al. (2020), the participation of banking industries in CSR would likely attract customers and employees. As a result, customer retention and employee satisfaction in CSR participation increases. Increasing customer retention and employee satisfaction positively contributes to the industry's sustainability. Hence, based on the analysis of Hussain et al. (2020), CSR has a direct relationship with customer retention, employee attraction and loyalty, enterprise reputation, and increasing social capital. Bonifácio Neto and Branco (2019) also previously attested to a correlation between CSR and banking sustainability, as further confirmed by Hussain et al. (2020) study. Most scholars have ambiguity in identifying the measuring approach of CSP. For instance, in the case of Hussain et al. (2020) and Bekele (2022), questionnaires are distributed to identify the perception of respondents and the impact on the operational and financial sustainability of the banking sector. Previous scholars under many studies have not identified quantitative metrics to measure CSP. Hence, looking at the investment in initiatives from Environment, Social, and Governance (ESG) dimensions, clients' social and financial inclusion can be used as the proxy measure of CSP in the banking industry.

Investment in Initiatives of Environment, Social, and Governance (ESG)

Kaplan, who introduced the concept and theories and measurements in the view of the Balanced Scorecard, calls the contemporary period of the market the Environment, Social, and Governance (ESG) era (Kaplan & McMillan, 2021). According to Sherwood and Pollard (2018), the United Nations introduced the Environment, Social, and Governance (ESG) initiatives as the principle for responsible investment (PRI) in 2006. The PRI encompassed six essential tenets. According to the guide, corporations are required to include ESG aspects in analysis and decisions while making investments. Besides, businesses abide by incorporating ESG in policy and application of business. Apart from a willingness to disclose ESG issues, companies must apply PRI principles in any investment. Lastly, corporations are expected to work on approaches to effectively implement PRI and report the performance to the institutions to which the sector is accountable (Sherwood & Pollard, 2018).

As recommended in the systematic review of literature by García-Pérez et al. (2017), checking the relationship between the dollars of investment on ESG initiatives and the sustainability of the banking industry is vital. Findings indicate that the regional proportion of investments implementing ESG initiatives following PRI varies from region to region. Globally, only 26 % of investment is aligned with the PRI principle, with the highest percentage coverage in Europe and Australia, respectively (Sherwood & Pollard, 2018). In African regions, as further studied by Sherwood and Pollard (2018), South Africa invested about 326 billion, while East African and Western African regions invested only 15 billion dollars and 12 billion dollars, respectively, based on the 2016 reports on ESG initiatives.

Financial and Social Inclusion: Percentage of Population Served and Vulnerable Population Served

Microfinance was introduced in the banking industry to provide financial services for people experiencing poverty. When raising the issue of inclusion, the initiative of CSR is related to the Diversity Equity and Inclusion (DEI) practice and implementation in the banking sector. The DEI concept and frameworks are mainly aligned with the civil rights movement and initiatives practiced by various industries to reduce inclusion challenges raised during the 1960s civil rights movement (Beavers, 2018). Loan disbursement of banks with the inclusion of a financially marginalized part of the community enhances the financial potential of a community. Among the recent studies, Gallego-Sosa et al. (2021) analyzed how banking services to women in Europe contributed to realizing the Sustainable Development Goals (SDG). Microfinance share companies should expand the outreach of financial inclusion by increasing the percentage of the population served under the banking programs, mainly focusing on gender-based service and encouraging vulnerable parts of society to enhance their financial capability. Such implementation can likely be considered as one part of CSR practice that attracts customers and increases the likelihood of operational and financial sustainability of banks (Gallego-Sosa et al., 2021).

Women's Financial Inclusion and Saving Performance of Microfinance

Building the customer base has a crucial impact on banking efficiency (Manirakiza, 2020). Most institutions with a stable customer base likely have better competitive power. The customer dimension under crucial performance indicators is measured in various approaches. According to Cornfield (2022), companies should identify the establishment purpose to grow as expected. As a banking industry, microfinance's role is to deliver financial opportunities for marginalized communities. Microfinance has the vision to reduce the poverty level of the clients. Hand in hand, banking industries offer financial opportunities to boost saving performance. Micro-credit organizations can meet growth expectations when simultaneously fulfilling consumer needs (Cornfield, 2022). Such firms running to optimize profitability need to have a global purpose. Besides, firms need a purpose for changing the lifestyle of customers and engaging customers in buying the products and services produced (Cornfield, 2022). In the case of banking industries, particularly microfinance, it has a global mandate to serve people experiencing poverty who do not have credit opportunities from traditional banks by providing small-size loans (Chikwira et al., 2022). A study on the impact of saving and small loan services of microfinance revealed that women's financial and social well-being is improved, and children's nutrition patterns have changed (Gichuru et al., 2019).

Women's empowerment in providing financial services has dual benefits: for the women and the institution. Financial inclusion by providing loan services for women has a positive contribution (Mengstie, 2022). The role of microfinance in such a regard is very significant. Microfinance enables women to boost their income and empowers women to own assets. Mengstie (2022) explains three significant areas where micro-credit institutions are involved. As women are empowered to get loan services, women's income increases alarmingly based on women's hard work and diligence in business activities. The increase in income further leads women to have an asset that may take the form of investment, either short-term or long-term. As women are likely to take risks to optimize their future return from investment due to loan service, the likelihood of women depositing high savings increases (Mengstie, 2022).

Microcredit and microfinance institutions focus on women's empowerment due to the perception that women have higher integrity for the repaying loans disbursed (Okesina, 2021). Despite various arguments on the goal of women-centered loan and saving programs, most scholars in previous studies support the claim that women's empowerment in micro-credit has a significant positive contribution to the saving of organizational performance of banking industries (Khursheed et al., 2021). Okesina (2021) criticizes the deliberate prioritization of women in loan service, claiming that microfinance institutions target women to benefit the institution, not the women. However, Okesina (2021) needs to quantify the contribution of microfinance in providing loan services and the profitability of the banking industry under the study. On the other side, scholars such as Daher et al. (2022) contend that women's saving empowerment significantly contributes to changing women's lives compared to financial inclusion by providing loan services to women. In the case of most microfinance industries, the saving performance of women is tracked and used as a baseline to set loan limits as women require loan disbursement (Daher et al., 2022). Contrary to traditional banks, microfinance has multi-dimensional saving and loan programs to empower women, in turn, to optimize the profitability and self-sufficiency of banking businesses.

Role of Women's Financial Inclusion in Performance of Loan Service and Institutional Stability

Women's financial inclusion significantly contributes to the microfinance industry's financial performance (Mia et al., 2021). When inclusion is referred to as providing financial opportunities such as paving the way for the process of loan service, such packages open the chance for women and vulnerable communities in loan service. Traditionally, microfinance institutions have provided greater attention to women since establishing micro-credit businesses. Based on Mia et al. (2021) study on 172 microfinance institutions in Eastern Europe and Central Asian Countries, women clients have significantly contributed to the organizational performance of loan services compared to male clients. The scholars contend that women had comparatively better integrity in utilizing the disbursed loan for the aimed purpose. According to Mia et al. (2021), the global proportion of women in microfinance comprises two-thirds of the total clients. The same is true for European and Asian-based microfinance. However, the reality varies from country to country, particularly in East African nations such as Ethiopia.

Women's financial inclusion in the microfinance industry contributed to narrowing the gender gap of empowerment (Roy & Patro, 2022). Reviewing 75 articles published within the last 21 years since 2000, Roy and Patro (2022) found that women's exclusion from loan services contributes to the gender gap. Among all the factors restraining women in financial inclusion is related to the women's demand to participate in business activities by taking loans from banking industries. According to Roy and Patro (2022), socioeconomic and cultural constraints were the determining factors. Roy and Patro's (2022) finding on the participation of women clients in loan services is far from the finding by Mia et al. (2021). The differences in scholars' arguments and empirical studies' findings are due to the difference in the scope and the data considered. For instance, in a study in Latin America and the Caribbean countries, out of 49% of women's clients, only 10% of women were considered for the loan service (Lazarte et al., 2022). Azar et al. (2018) relate the poor performance of banking industries in providing loan services for women in Latin America and the Caribbean countries to the level of knowledge and willingness of women to be part of loan services. According to Azar et al. (2018) and Lazarte et al. (2022), financial industries in the examined area are reluctant to provide loan services for women in fear of risk.

Perrin and Weill's (2022) study found a negative relationship between the gender gap and the financial performance of institutions under the study. Perrin and Weill (2022) recommended providing a relatively higher loan service for females than for males. The justification of Perrin and Weill (2022) is that the scholars found that women have shown better loan repayment than men. As loan repayment is the most significant factor affecting the ability of the financial industries to have enough capital and potential to provide loan services, women's inclusion in loan service has a positive contribution when a loan is disbursed subject to the literacy level and willingness and commitment of borrowers to repay (Lazarte et al., 2022; Perrin & Weill, 2022). Perrin and Weill (2022) state that women's financial inclusion in loan services positively impacts financial self-sufficiency and institutional longevity.

Business Agility Metrics

The term agility may have various meanings depending on the context. Business agility is to respond comprehensively to a changing and unpredictable environment (Goldman et al., 1995). Accordingly, the agility concept encompasses organizational agility and employee agility. At a corporate level, as the business motive is to maximize profitability, agile organizations operate in the best possible way to optimize profitability while simultaneously changing approaches to meet customer expectations. From the human resource point of view, employee agility enhances business agility when the human and technological resources are organized to respond quickly to emerging needs. The competitive nature of domestic and international markets calls for agility in a business. According to Goldman et al. (1995), a successful company competes in profitability, market share, and customer satisfaction.

Agility is about working to the best of the operations and innovation (Rigby et al., 2020). Rigby et al. (2020) compare oil and vinegar with agility and bureaucracy. Accordingly, as oil and vinegar do not mix easily, the same is valid for agility and bureaucracy. For a better result, an agile company works in an ambidextrous approach, working on existing operations and innovation. Hence, agility also relates to business adaptability in leadership and culture, team organization, scale, and adoption of improved business models and practices. Based on Rigby et al. (2020), agility has various dimensions. For instance, an agile business system is neither static nor chaotic but flexible and adaptive in organizational management.

In agile business, firms have shared corporate purpose and values. Strategies of agile business are adaptive. Through a learning process, agile companies change the leadership approach and culture. As there is collaborative team spirit in the working environment of agile firms, the business operation works in an integrated way (Rigby et al., 2020). Agility is also tied to leadership style. Rigby et al. (2020) claim that applying Beedle et al. (2001) agile manifesto would likely install agile leadership in businesses.

The manifesto by the software research development team recommends teamwork, striving to find a working solution, accepting customer feedback, and responding to changes. From the Chief Executive Officers' standpoint, agile business leaders work more on strategy than operations (Rigby et al., 2020).

Dimensions of Agility and Cash Flow as A Proxy Measure

The approach to measuring the agility of a business may take various forms—Goldman et al. (1995) rate firms' agility in percentage based on four primary areas. The first dimension is the customer's, evaluating customer satisfaction with the produced goods and services. Such dimension coincides with the customer dimension of the Balanced Scorecard of Kaplan and McMillan (2021). The third and fourth dimensions focus on handling unforeseen events organizationally and from a human resource aspect. However, the second dimension focuses on the competitiveness of the firm. Goldman et al. (1995) approach of measuring business agility using scores in percentage may work if a survey questionnaire is distributed to measure the level. The method would have a subjective but not objective evaluation. Hence, the problem calls for an alternative approach.

Based on Edmondson and Gulati's (2021) approach to agility hacks, saving corporate accounts during a crisis is considered the best approach to agile leadership. During an unforeseen and unpredictable time, looking at the balance sheet accounts about the cash flow is more relevant than the profit and loss or income statement (Freakley & Donahue, 2022). Simultaneously, using existing finance to rotate in the best way to invest in innovative ideas and long-run opportunities is recommended to realize agile leadership in banking industries.

The cash flow informs the resource flexibility in the banking sector. As Stobierski (2020) stated, the financial dimension of profitability indicates the number of dollars left for the business after paying all expenses. However, cash flow is the difference between cash in and out in a given period. While a positive cash flow indicates that a higher amount of cash is moving into the bank, a negative cash flow indicates that a more elevated amount is moving out. In times of uncertainty, organizations better have a positive cash flow to the business and can invest in opportunities. Financial health would be in danger when banking industries face a negative cash flow during an unpredictable time. To solve the problem of business agility in retail banking, Smart et al. (2019) check organizational performance and work by starting from small to big scale and building robust and agile leadership. As a result, Aghina et al. (2021) attested that business agility in customer satisfaction, employee engagement, and operational performance would significantly improve firms' financial health.

Savings For Cash Flow and Business Agility of Microfinance

Revenue diversification has a significant role in maintaining the financial health of microfinance and banks (Githaiga, 2021). There are various incomes or revenue for the banking industries. According to Al-Azzam (2019), savings are a microfinance institution's leading source of loanable funds. Apart from savings, microfinance uses subsidies from the public and nongovernmental organizations. Accordingly, as Githaiga (2021) stated, diversifying the revenue channels enhances banks' financial stability instead of solely emphasizing a single source of income. Likewise, in microfinance, banking institutions such as micro-credit, cooperatives, credit units, and commercial banks benefited from income diversification to use as loanable funds.

Since the establishment of microfinance, microfinance institutions have served low-income groups by supplying micro-saving, micro-credit, and micro-insurance (Jalil, 2021). Micro-saving has played a significant role in the growth and development of microfinance institutions. According to Jalil (2021), micro-saving participants played a dual role. First, as the firms save in microfinance, the entrepreneurial potential to invest in alternative forms of investment increases. Second, the cash saved in microfinance by the entrepreneurs helped as a source of loan to lend as a micro-credit. Empirical studies attest that saving has a solid positive significant relation with credit access (Anane et al., 2021). Such results inform how microfinance traditionally works to serve clients by using deposits as a source of loan disbursement.

From the empirical standpoint, funding sources also have a crucial impact based on the previous 170 research findings on the determining factors of microfinance self-sufficiency and performance by Hermes & Hudon (2018). However, as stated by scholars, the pattern of organizational performance varies from country to country. In the case of using savings as a source of funds for micro-credit, microfinance industries would have a greater outreach based on saving performance. Based on Rosengard's (2022) study about Bank Rakyat Indonesia (BRI), the microbank has revealed a significant exemplary performance in financial inclusion since 1895. Reviewing the status of the bank, the bank is amongst the largest diversified microbanks in Indonesia with a 113-billion-dollar asset. From the profitability dimension, the bank recorded a 2.2 billion dollar profit. Besides leadership, innovation, and fin-tech adoption, the micro bank has intensified its networks with 179 million savings accounts. Based on the study by Rosengard (2022), the micro-credit opportunity in 2021 increased by seven times compared to 1990. As the study reports, 13.2 million borrowers got a chance to get financial opportunities due to a dramatic increase in the source of funds from savings (Rosengard, 2022).

Precautionary savings helped small enterprises during COVID-19 (Cowling et al., 2020). The recent financial shock due to the pandemic put institutions at risk due to the lockdowns and the stop of normal business operations. The business closure during the pandemic negatively affected financial health institutions, particularly individuals and firms. The same was true for micro-credit industries. However, individuals and small-scale industries with prior precautionary savings for unprecedented and unforeseen financial risk helped the depositors and the cash flow in microfinance. A recent study revealed that over 60 percent of businesses had cash shortages. However, 40 percent of businesses under the study helped banking institutions to become relatively self-reliant (Cowling et al., 2020). Such experience has taught agile businesses and microfinance to manage the cash flow for a "rainy day" (Cowling et al., 2020, p-584).

The Relationship Between Return on Asset and Cash Flow

As the return on asset is the ratio of net income to total assets, the positive or negative influence of return on asset is mainly determined by the banking industry's profitability (Frisch, 2014). From the most common key performance indicators financial firms use, profitability ratios are essential in tracking organizational financial status. Among the financial dimensions included in Kaplan and Norton's (1992) model and the recent model encompassing the environmental, social, and governance era, profitability measures such as return on asset talk more about the financial trend of businesses (Kaplan & McMillan, 2021). In banking industries such as microfinance, there are additional profitability metrics such as Return on Deposits (ROD) and Return on Loan (ROL) as a measure of profitability (Kolawole, 2020).

The level of cash flow impacts the profitability of microfinance (Smart et al., 2019; Stobierski, 2020). Empirical evidence from the recent study by Kolawole (2020) shows that return on deposits and loans positively contribute to the net income. The higher the numerator of the return on asset ratio, the higher the return on asset, positively contributing to the institution's overall financial well-being. From a banking industry perspective, the higher the savings deposit, the higher the institution's financial status. However, as clients' withdrawal of savings increases, frequent withdrawal of savings may deteriorate the financial potential of the lending institution (Kolawole, 2020). Henceforth, higher profitability indicates a higher cash inflow and results in the potential to boost the business agility of the firm.

Recent research evidence on the financial performance of banks revealed that cash flow has a positive relationship with the financial performance of banks and insurance (Said & Doll, 2021). As the cash flow level of an institution informs analysts about the liquidity level, the higher inflow of cash results in higher profitability. However, as the outflow increases, financial well-being will be negatively affected. Unless a higher inflow of cash is invested in having a higher return, holding a mere large amount of cash may negatively affect the financial status of the banking business unless invested appropriately. Hence, the influence of cash flow on the business's profitability is determined by effective cash management (Said & Doll, 2021). Appropriate investment positively affects banks' operating efficiency and financial status. Such results can be realized by reducing operating expenses and managing costs (Mehzabin et al., 2022).

Lean Banking Metrics

The concept of lean leadership and management goes back to the 1950s. The term lean was introduced by engineer Taiichi Ohno, who created the Toyota Production System (Womack & Jones, 1996). Lean thinking aims to reduce waste from manufacturing operations (Womack & Jones, 1996; Womack et al., 2007). The idea relates not solely to waste reduction but also to boosting operational efficiency. As lean eliminates processes that do not add value, the concept may have a significant relationship with the Balanced Scorecard's improved business process dimension. Simultaneously, as lean business implementation considers enabling the human resource to act on change, there is a significant relationship with business agility. As Blank (2013) stated, the agility of the business is essential to implement a lean approach. According to Blank (2013), leanness relies on the business model, customer development, and agile development. The interrelation implies how Balanced Scorecard dimensions of business processes and customer dimensions are indispensable to achieve the expected lean banking.

Literature supports lean thinking and approach in operation are considered part of change management (Errida & Lotfi, 2021). Scholars argue that a lean system improves organizational performance in optimizing business operations. Such results can be achieved by organizations not introducing the Toyota Production System or lean system (Chandrasekaran & Toussaint, 2019). However, business leaders at various managerial levels should have the knowledge and leadership role in implementing the approach from the planning to the implementation stage of operational and strategic activities.

Cost-to-Income Ratio

According to Domenech et al. (2020) study of Latin American banking operations, cost/ spending should be appropriately managed by financial industries to work at optimum or minimum cost. The scholars claim that an actual minimum cost limit impacts financial well-being, productivity, and sustainability in a competitive money market. A percentage reduction in the total cost of the capital building, indirect cost, IT-related cost, administrative cost, marketing cost, and others would save financial potential by 20 to 30 percent. To work at an optimum cost, Domenech et al. (2020) suggest assessing areas of improvement, designing an implementation plan to prioritize activities, and transforming the business system by implementing lean leadership. In lean management, cost-to-income should be optimized. As the denominator of the cost-to-income ratio is lower than the numerator, a business's financial health would be adversely affected. However, as the operating cost is lower than income, the metrics indicate a lower cost level required to earn a higher income, further informing analysts about operational efficiency.

Alternatively, as a proxy measure of lean management, the efficiency ratio can be used as an alternative measure calculated by dividing operating expenses by total revenue. From a traditional definition standpoint of efficiency, Mankins (2017) states that efficiency is all about executing operational activities with less. The definition of efficiency in the examined literature is tied to the resources required for operation. As efficiency is seen from cost and operating expenditure, analysts can further consider the ratio of the number of clients served to the total number of employees. As banking industries are efficient in cost, expenditure, and helping loan and saving clients, the likelihood of sustainability of banking firms would increase (Mankins, 2017).

Operational Efficiency: Percentage of Loan Repaid

A higher percentage of loans repaid is a good indicator of operational efficiency in the banking industry. Though there is no standard to differentiate the best level of operational efficiency using a percentage of loans repaid, some banks use a rule of thumb such as attaining 95 % of loans repaid (Schlesinger, 2021). Karlan et al. (2016) suggest microfinance to work on improving saving performance, digital financial services, and insurance. Simultaneously, exemplary banking industries are recognized by the high repayment. Hence, a higher repayment percentage indicates effective microfinance (Karlan et al., 2016).

The Contribution of Performance in Loan Repayment

Loan defaulting and loan delinquency hurt the overall performance of microfinance institutions (Chong, 2021; Endris, 2022). As there is poor performance in loan repayment, for instance, the debt-to-equity ratio would be higher, negatively affecting the financial health of banking industries. From the borrower side, the loan repayment behavior of consumers depends on the spending pattern. For instance, small-scale enterprises with poor spending behavior have difficulty repaying loans timely. The reverse is true for firms with a planned spending and loan management system. Businesses that invest in non-income-generating packages find it hard to repay loans (Chong, 2021; Endris, 2022).

According to Chong (2021), loan management and self-discipline of borrowers determine the likelihood of loan repayment. From the side of the lending institution, poor follow-up and monitoring systems may lead to higher loan defaulting (Endris, 2022). The institution's financial health would be severely affected because loan repayment is linked to credit risk. In most cases of microfinance, the funds revolve from consumer to consumer. The saving and loan repayment performance determines the institution's current and future financial state and potential to make loan plans (Chong, 2021). Pre-screening of borrowers and strong credit management are crucial to mitigate the challenges related to poor performance in loan repayment (Chong, 2021; Endris, 2022).

Recent studies on determining repayment factors revealed that leadership from both the borrowers and lending institutions determines the possibility of loan repayment (Balvanz et al., 2019). As borrowers have prior experience in undertaking planned business and cost-effective spending behavior, the potential to repay would be boosted. Simultaneously, as the borrowers have a skill set in planning, financial management, and literacy, their motivation and awareness positively contribute to loan repayment. From the side of microfinance and banking industries, for successful loan repayment performance, the banking industries should provide training to reduce the adverse effect of late repayment on the institution's financial health (Balvanz et al., 2019).

A study on 175 micro enterprises revealed how loan repayment period and timeliness of loan influence the loan repayment performance (Kiros, 2023). Kiros (2023) recommends a shorter repayment period for better repayment performance. Besides, microfinance industries need to adopt a tracking and loan management system assisted by information technology to collect dispersed loans. If loan repayment challenges are minimized to the best extent, lending institutions will have abundant capital. Simultaneously, if borrowers do not spend the loan appropriately in a planned way for the intended target, the profitability of an individual business and the lender would be negatively affected. Such challenges may lead microfinance industries to a shortage of finance and severely affect the business operation and process of expanding the outreach (Kiros, 2023).

Number of Loanees and Loan Repayment on Banking Leanness

The customer dimension is an operational metric to measure customer satisfaction among the four BSC dimensions (Kaplan & McMillan, 2021; Refera, 2020). As Kaplan and McMillan (2021) stated, the objective of an institution measuring the customer dimension is to evaluate the satisfaction level of customers. From an economic point of view, the interests and objectives of customers versus firms vary. While customers such as depositors and loanees or beneficiaries of loans aim to maximize satisfaction, the banking industries aim to optimize profitability. As there are times when banking industries take a calculated risk, unfavorable risk due to low repayment rates may discourage microfinance from disbursing much money for disloyal clients. Such a measure of financial industries is to mitigate risk related to losses and higher service costs (Kaplan & Mikes, 2014). Operational efficiency, measured by the cost-to-income ratio, can be adversely affected due to losses (Mankins, 2017; Domenech et al., 2020). Hence, traditionally lean banks are cautious when disbursing loans.

Without careful pre-evaluation and screening of beneficiaries, the loan repayment performance would be riskier (Kaplan & Mikes, 2014; Refera, 2020). Kaplan and Mikes (2014) categorize risk as preventable, strategic, and external. Accordingly, most operational-related risks can be prevented by managers. Strategic risk is when managers decide to take a higher risk, expecting a higher return in the future. A manager may not easily control external risks. In the case of microfinance loan services, there are two-sided challenges: customer-based and administrative. The number of beneficiaries may outweigh the available resources. On such occasions, hand in hand with managers, loan officers must carefully select eligible loanees. As stated by Balvanz et al. (2019), the skill of loanees may influence the likelihood of loan repayment. Simultaneously, the literacy level of the beneficiaries influences their ability to manage the disbursed loan (Hernandez et al., 2018). As a lean manager, to minimize cost and optimize the return from loan disbursement, a credit scoring model may help to decide eligible loanees (Medina-Olivares et al., 2021). However, in most developing nations, as the credit scoring approach is yet to be adopted as a system of loan management, the operational efficiency of microfinance can be affected negatively due to the adverse effect of low loan repayment. External factors such as climate and financial shocks may also ruin the repaying ability of borrowers (Kaplan & Mikes, 2014). The number of loanees should be carefully determined for higher-expected loan repayment.

Predictive Modeling and Research Analysis in Business

The concept of predictive modeling was introduced initially by Galton (1889). Some scholars argue that in the 1990s, a mathematics scholar group named the Data Abstraction Research Group (DARG) first developed and introduced a predictive modeling and analysis approach (Apte et al., 2003). A linear or non-linear regression model is employed depending on the nature of the relationship of variables included in the study to undertake business prediction. Besides, assumptions and theoretical bases determine the type of regression model selection. Galton introduced the concept of regression, intending to model how independent variables influence the dependent variable statistically and mathematically. The main aim of regression models is to check if statistical evidence supports theoretical claims and assumptions. The other name of the independent variable is a predictor variable, indicating that the dependent variable is predicted based on response or independent variables (Ramachandran & Tsokos, 2020). Inferential statistics were initially used to determine the genetic relationship and predict based on regression models (Galton, 1889). Later, regression models were used in various fields.

The regression model of prediction encompasses hypothesis testing, including a sample dataset, and checking whether the data fits the selected mathematical model (Ramachandran & Tsokos, 2020). Because of the relevance of datasets in predictive modeling and analysis, businesses started using the approach to make data-driven decision-making. Multinational corporations and government agencies are the prominent users. The value of data is realized when used for prediction. For better prediction and analysis, using a combination of models is recommended (Page, 2018). Nowadays, businesses hire data engineers and specialists to benefit from the data and make future predictions. Data quality is another factor influencing predictability (Redman, 2018). In regression and predictive modeling, researchers need first to identify the specific objective of undertaking the study. Specifying the study's objective helps to identify relevant data on variables that should be included in the study. Second, the data quality should be tested before regression analysis, and remedial measures must be taken. In general, to make future predictions that are viable and accurate, appropriate statistical procedures should be followed to check the data quality (Redman, 2018).

Businesses use predictive modeling to assess the future behavior of customers and make proactive decisions for optimizing the objective of profit maximization and cost minimization (Karlan & Luca, 2022; Redman, 2018). Thinking about the future is linked with businesses' objectives of sustainability and self-sufficiency. The need for businesses' future sustainability and financial stability made predictive modeling valuable science. As a data-driven manager, using data to understand the relationship between business variables is critical (Karlan & Luca, 2022). For instance, correlation analysis and predictive models help in identifying relationships. If an appropriate regression procedure is employed, there are two main benefits. As Karlan and Luca (2022) stated, predictive models inform about the future behavior of variables. The information could be either the statistical direction or the extent to which response variables influence the predictor variable. The basis for the prediction is the historical data collected (Davenport & Fitts, 2021). Using descriptive statistics about the variables employed in the study or advanced predictive modeling such as Structural Equation Modeling, sufficient data should be collected in a reasonable time (Davenport & Fitts, 2021). For better statistical precision and estimation, including more relevant data helps build the model (Wieckowski, 2021). Apart from using predictive modeling for future prediction, unknown variables that need attention can be examined using predictive modeling (Biçer et al., 2022). As businesses are in an uncertain competitive environment, employing predictive modeling to understand the future of business in the research and development department contributes a lot.

Business analytics and intelligence paved the way for predictive modeling in the age of Artificial Intelligence automated machine learning-based prediction (Abrantes & Ostergaard, 2022; Siegel, 2020a). As a researcher, as checking the data quality is relevant for appropriate precision, data should be used according to research ethics and national and international standards. Consent forms should be collected from study participants to verify that the participants are selected with voluntariness (Siegel, 2020a). Besides, data collected from participants should not be misused as such conduct fails to protect the data privacy rule of research (Abrantes & Ostergaard, 2022).

The Role and Application of Forecasting in Business

Forecasting the future is vital to prepare for the forthcoming ups and downs (Rinne, 2021). As business patterns change daily and every moment, the fluctuations influence organizations' performance. Hence, the turbulences and booms need to be appropriately managed. The failure to proactively act on the alarming challenges of businesses is related to a failure to plan. Waiting till adverse impacts are prevalent on financial and operational organizational performance results in higher risk. Rinne (2021) calls the reactive approach a defensive and recommends a proactive approach to solving organizational problems at the right time. As businesses live in a more uncertain market, to address future challenges, managers need guiding principles to audit the present performance and design a scientific strategy to tackle challenges (Rinne, 2021). Before designing a strategy, understanding how forecasting has the potential to inform leaders about the expected trends, either troughs or booms, is relevant.

The preparation of a scientific forecast requires critical procedures. In corporate industries, forecasting has various valid objectives. According to Foley and Khavkin

(2019), projections help identify resource needs based on the context. Projection is also about a pathway for future areas of growth. Besides, forecasting encompasses identifying alternative areas of competition in a dynamic market. Understanding the reality based on historical data helps not only project the future financial health but also to identify non-financial areas of work such as leadership and soft skills required to compete in the market. Corporations must apply forecasting models for a targeted plan to work in the next three to five years (Foley & Khavkin, 2019).

The baseline of forecasting starts from operational activities (Foley & Khavkin, 2019). Banking industries rely on saving and operational activities on loan services. Operational activities such as an increase in the number of depositors and loanees likely increase the financial flow of currency in the money market. Looking at the trends of operational-organizational performance, managers can design additional programs. The historical insights inform the prevailing situation. Based on the trends, managers can identify and address areas of improvement. In addition, predictions also guide businesses to identify approaches to growth and plan resource requirements for better performance. In predictive modeling, the rates of changes due to an increase or decrease in a variable's value and the negative and positive signs associated with the coefficients of independent variables tell the reader about the potential dynamics in the future (Foley & Khavkin, 2019). Thinking at the margin, managers can predict the effect of a change in one or more of the operational-strategic areas on the predictor of financial performance (Mize et al., 2019). Hence, a marginal effect or rate of change of a variable may determine the competitive power of a business and further inform leaders about the challenges the company is facing (Foley & Khavkin, 2019; Mankins & Gottfredson, 2022).

Among the prediction areas of business, research, and development, departments of firms predict employee performance (Ingram & Choi, 2022). One area of human resource management, such as turnover, influences organizational performance (Zhao et al., 2018). In statistical terms, there are mediating variables between turnover and organizational performance. For instance, to identify if variables such as managerial interaction, packages of benefit to employee physical and mental wellbeing, and type of leadership of an organization can directly influence the turnover rate. As a result, turnover may adversely affect organizational performance (Tupper & Ellis, 2022). However, employee satisfaction reduces the turnover rate. Suppose business analysts go further to identify potential variables contributing to organizational performance. In that case, some theories support teamwork, effective communication, Equity, Diversity, and Inclusion (EDI) as determining factors of organizational progress (Corritore et al., 2020; Ingram & Choi, 2022). Such empirical findings and testable assumptions and premises are the results of prediction.

According to Kenny (2021), predictive modeling in business is not only about evaluating the past. However, predictions help how Key Performance Indicators (KPIs) relate to each other. Commonly, corporate managers use KPIs to evaluate the past and current progress of the organization in various key dimensions. Using past and recent reports and data, business researchers can predict the future of a business to undertake data-driven decision-making, to continue or stop working at a loss for a particular period. For instance, during COVID-19, some firms continued to work regardless of financial, supply, and demand shock. Businesses that extract opportunities during times of unprecedented financial turbulence can decide to work in consideration of business opportunities in times of challenge and take advantage (Fairlie, 2020). Such a business decides to work regardless of losses when having an optimistic prediction.

Researchers in leadership and organizational management use prediction to evaluate leaders' and managers' potential (Intagliata et al., 2022). Leadership potential relates to the ability of managers and leaders with the required leadership skills (Robel, 2022). According to Intagliata et al. (2022), measurable behaviors associated with the best leadership skills contribute to building bright and strong future leaders. Past data about leaders' skills and potential should be assessed to check the strengths and weaknesses and predict the likelihood of future leaders' prevalence. Researchers evaluate leadership strength based on proxy measures of leadership traits. Apart from identifying leadership skill proxy variables, in a working environment, critical factors are associated with leadership quality (Praslova, 2023). Corporations investing in human capital get information on the bottlenecks and direct the case to higher-level managers to work on investing in an additional training program. Later, managers plan and design training programs to fill the gap in the sector, which is realized due to predictive modeling (Intagliata et al., 2022).

Despite the role of prediction in business for centuries, the accuracy of prediction of businesses is endangered due to unprecedented and catastrophic worldwide impacts (Reeves et al., 2023). The volatility of the market leads to inaccuracies in predictions. Among the inaccuracies, there are exaggerated predictions (Suh, 2019). According to Suh (2019), such inaccuracies happen not because of automated machine learning-assisted statistical packages. However, people may report inflated data purposefully. Such practices violate research ethics and legal standards.

Summary and Transition

The review of the literature chapter introduces previously published scholarly articles on the success metrics associated with organizational performance based on the Balanced Scorecard approach and their respective relationship with the sustainability of banking industries such as microfinance, micro-credit, and banks. The literature review assessed in chapter 2 helps to understand the existing research gap in the study. Based on the review, prior scholars have tried to encompass financial metrics, customer service metrics, learning and growth dimensions, business process dimensions, and the relationship among the proxy variables included in the four significant prospects of a Balanced Scorecard. However, studies indicated in the review inform the need for in-depth research in identifying how business agility, leanness, and Corporate Social Responsibility initiatives relate to the well-being of financial sectors. Hence, the study pursues to fill the gap in the literature by testing for correlations between the variables under the study and help future researchers develop a predictive model and comprehensive customized Balanced Scorecard for banking industries in the Economic Social and Governance (ESG) and digital era. Chapter 3 portrays the research method of the study. Chapter 3 comprises the research design, data collection, and analysis method.

Chapter 3: Research Method and Design

Purpose Statement

The purpose of this study was two-fold. The primary purpose was to assess and test the relationship between business agility and leanness, CSR practice, and the BSC dimensions: customer, financial, learning and growth, and business process. If a relationship exists, the study further tests the relationship's strength and direction to establish comprehensive extended performance metrics and help future researchers build a predictive model to track the performance of the Omo microfinance institution. The study targeted Omo Bank in southern Ethiopia, focusing on ten branches of Sawla Omo microfinance at the Gofa Zone administration. The study tried to identify and examine additional variables associated with microfinance performance and the challenge of self-sufficiency. The variables included are the observed variables related to the four dimensions of BSC: business agility, leanness, and Corporate Social Responsibility (CSR). The observed variables for the latent or unobserved variables include Operating Self-Sufficiency (OSS), Return on Asset (ROA), Number of Depositors (CSSV) and Number of Loanee (CSLn), Number of New Borrowers (B), Number of Loan Officers (LnO), Employment Turnover Rate (ETR), Number of Women Loan Beneficiaries (WPn), Cash Flow (CshF) and Loan Repaid (LnRd). Based on theoretical literature, OSS depends on all the remaining explanatory variables.

The study utilized a quantitative research method. The study participants, the managerial bodies, and the employees working on the banking system extracted existing data from the internal database. The researcher worked on mining relevant variables to examine the trends and relationships among the selected variables. Moreover, the study encompassed quantitative operational and financial data trends within the recent five years, from 2019 to 2023. A correlational research design was used to conduct the study. The study incorporates a longitudinal dataset (Goldberger, 1972). Hence, the correlational research design suits studies interested in understanding the strength and direction of relationships among variables (Cho et al., 2022; Hair & Sarstedt, 2019; Zyphur et al., 2022). The study would contribute to identifying how banking industries play a substantial role in the financial inclusion of women and other vulnerable parts of the community for the benefit of organizational performance and stewardship initiatives. Besides, the study provided insights and knowledge on how banking participation in corporate social responsibility, business agility, and lean banking pave the way for the success of the banking industry.

Role of the Researcher

In most action research studies, researchers have an insider role (Herr & Anderson, 2015). Such an approach was used in this study. The insider role of the researcher is vital as the researcher has prior knowledge about the institution. Besides, a researcher's insider role eases data collection (Wilson et al., 2022). A reliable data collection instrument was employed to secure the privacy of the data collected from the institution's banking system. As a result, the data would be protected from unauthorized access to participants' identifiers in the data set (McKibbin et al., 2021). Besides, the data was managed by coding following a meaningful category subject to available research theories linked with variables (Allen, 2017). In the process, the confidentiality of the dataset was preserved. As the expected data would not have to identify names of persons and institutions affiliated with the study area, the report and analysis were presented anonymously. The researcher has no relationship with the institution. However, as the researcher used to work in the institution ten years ago, prior exposure to financial terminologies may support analyzing the report accurately and in the best possible way to make the reader understand the findings and discussion. The research scope was limited to ten branches of Sawla District Omo Bank for the convenience of data collection. The practitioner respects the NCBI's (1979) Belmont Report protocol by protecting the study's participants' personal information and protecting the human subjects. Peer-reviewed articles are used to write the literature. Similarly, credible scholarly publications supported findings during discussion and analysis that reflect the study's quality (Chong & Mason, 2021).

Participants

Since the study focused on understanding the relationship between business agility, lean banking, CSR, and the four dimensions of BSC in developing nations, the Omo Bank in Ethiopia, East Africa, is an appropriate geographic region. The region was purposively selected among the Sub-Saharan African Microfinance as prior researchers revealed the prevalence of a challenge of operational self-sufficiency and sustainability (Remer & Kattilakoski, 2021). Due to the unique success stories aligned to Omo Microfinance's transition from a microfinance industry to a bank, the researcher selected the specific bank to understand what performance indicators contributed to the industry's success in the money market (Omo Bank, 2023a). The population under investigation was Ethiopia's southern region, focusing on Omo microfinance banking industry clients, employees, and managerial bodies. As the study employed purposive sampling, the population selection is aligned with the method of sampling (Bridier, 2021).

The study encompasses variables related to clients and working employees. Based on the theories related to business agility, lean banking, CSR, and the four dimensions of BSC, women population (WPN), number of depositors (CSSV), and loanees (CSLN) were considered to understand the operational performance of the study area. Besides, employee turnover (ETR) was also assessed to understand how employee satisfaction relates to other indices. Loan repaid (LNRD), operational self-sufficiency (OSS), return on asset (ROA), and business process (BP) were the selected variables to understand organizational performance from various dimensions. The number of clients and employees fluctuated each quarter from 2019 to 2023. Hence, the study considers all data points across the nineteen quarters for the selected variables. The study does not involve human participants. However, the researcher has contact with the Omo bank, the research partner, not the people in the financial and operational accounts. The organization was formally requested by encrypted email to access information about the clients, managers, and financial and operational data from branches and the district. The district manager working on the internal banking system in the sector cooperated in providing relevant data associated with the selected dependent and independent variables. For the feasibility of data sending and receiving, encrypted email communication was considered to keep data security and ethical standards of research (Akanksha et al., 2022). As the data was not publicly available, a non-data disclosure and data use agreement with district microfinance was established. However, as the study is solely an academic paper, to enhance the academic credit and boost the competition effect of the research, the data might be disclosed, removing identifiers as per the data sharing and disclosure agreement

(Kwon & Motohashi, 2021). A positive working relationship with the district manager of

the institution was considered to keep the ethical standards of academic research.

Figure 1.

Sample Location Map

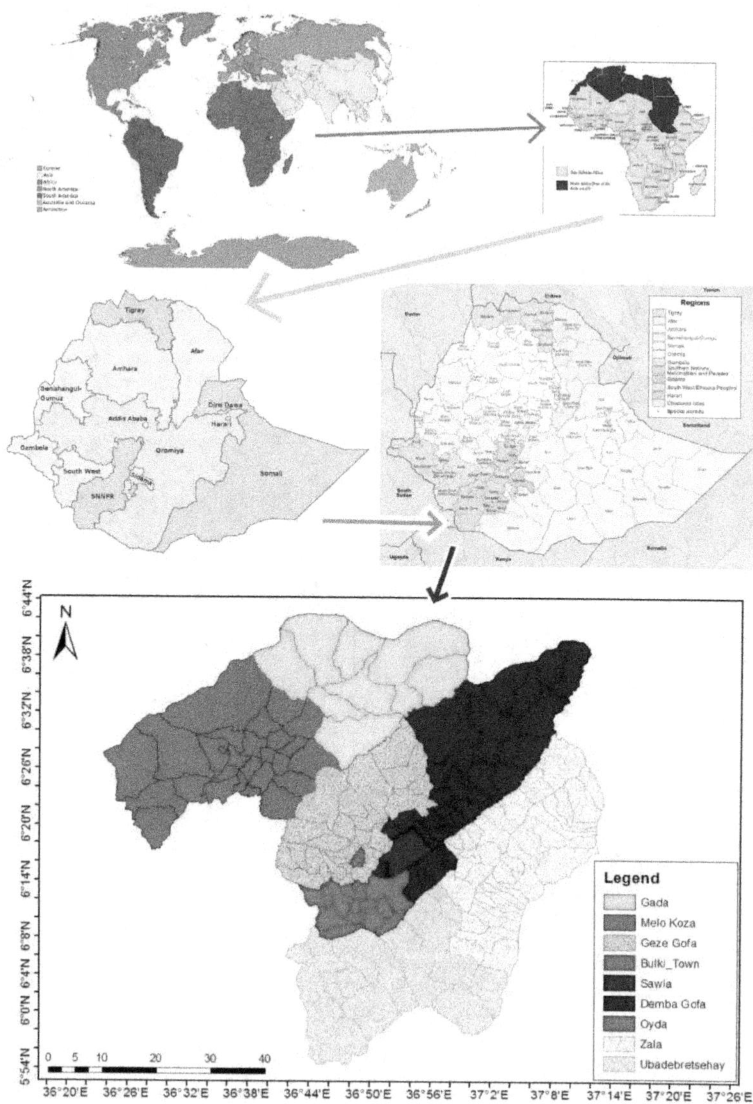

Source: Ngoran et al., 2016; Blanc, 2023; Gofa Zone Administration, 2023; Wikimedia, 2023; Wikimedia, 2023a

Research Method

The study used the quantitative research method. A quantitative research method was used to identify the relationships between business agility, lean banking, CSR, and the four dimensions of BSC. The justification for selecting a quantitative research methodology is that collecting objective quantitative data helps generalize and make a data-driven prediction (Creswell & Creswell, 2017). However, in the qualitative research method, as the variables employed are not quantifiable, the nature of the data type hardens the process of correlational analysis. In the quantitative approach, hypothesized claims can be tested; in qualitative research, claims cannot be tested, and no statistical imputation is used. The quantitative research method is relevant as the study employed hypotheses to be tested that match the data pattern (Frost, 2020). A quantitative research method best suits the research study focusing on inferential statistics. Correlational analysis in quantitative research is objective; however, the subjective nature of the qualitative analysis is vulnerable to biased conclusions and estimates that cannot be tested (Render et al., 2018). In addition, as the study solely considers quantified operational and financial organizational performance of banking industries, the qualitative approach is unsuitable for this study. Besides, the quantitative approach was selected for replicability, which broadens the chance of external researchers to test the validity of the research. In the case of a qualitative research method, research analysis can be done based on participants' perception and perspective; however, quantitative studies do not follow such an approach as the qualitative study (Creswell & Creswell, 2017; Easterby-Smith et al., 2018; Hoy & Adams, 2016).

Research Design

The study used a correlational research design. A correlational analysis would test the relationship between the identified variables related to business agility, lean banking, CSR, and the four dimensions of BSC. As Creswell and Creswell (2017) stated, such design helps measure the degree of relationship and understand the relationship between individual variables and the direction of the relationship. The quantitative research method has two different approaches to prediction: the correlational method and the time series method (Render et al., 2018). In the case of the correlational prediction method, researchers assume a statistically significant relationship between the selected variables. The correlational research design intends to identify the direct or inverse relationship among the selected variables. However, in the case of a time series predictive research design model, the objective is to predict the value of a variable in the future based on historical trends (Render et al., 2018). This research study aimed to look at how business agility, banking leanness, and dimensions of corporate social responsibility relate to the four dimensions of the BSC. The correlational research design is appropriate for such a study. In addition, the use of parametric or non-parametric correlational tests and analysis is relevant to answer the research question of to what extent the dimensions of the Balanced Scorecard relate to business agility (BA), lean banking (LB), and CSR initiatives in Sawla District Omo Bank (Cho et al., 2022; Goldberger, 1972; Hair & Sarstedt, 2019; Zyphur et al., 2022).

Population and Sampling

Omo microfinance was established on August 14, 1996, in Southern Ethiopia, East Africa. Among the seventeen Districts of Omo Bank (2023), the Sawla district was purposively selected. The study area was purposively selected among the newly established banks since the Omo bank was the only bank in the Gofa Zonal administration that started as a microfinance and later grew into a corporate bank. As the study aimed to understand the relationship between business agility, banking leanness, CSR, and the BSC dimensions, selecting such a newly established bank might tell the relationship among the selected variables and understand how the selected variables contributed to OSS and growth from microfinance to a competitive bank.

Previous studies on Omo microfinance in the Southern region revealed challenges related to loan repayment, financial outreach, and organizational performance (Ashenafi, 2018; Ayele & Goshu, 2018; Dangisso & Deyganto, 2020; Kebede & Regassa, 2019; Melese & Asfaw, 2019; Mohammed & Wobe, 2019). However, the examined Omo microfinance is no longer microfinance but is officially among Ethiopian banks registered by the National Bank of Ethiopia. Such a dramatic move in the decade triggered the researcher to study the bank, explicitly employing purposive sampling. The justification for purposive sampling is that the researcher specifically selected the study scope to understand and learn how emerging banks have grown from microfinance to a bank. Such deliberate, judgmental, and purposive sampling techniques are best suited when the target population is small and if the researcher has prior knowledge that the target population best suits answering the proposed research question. Besides, as the researcher expects to get real-time data and has prior knowledge about the topic and trend of data collection in the study area, purposive sampling is appropriate for selecting a convenient sample from an existing dataset (Bhardwaj, 2019).

The selected purposive sampling approach paves the way to minimize the costs of the research and the time required to finish the study (Dudovskiy, 2022). As the study has no funding source, purposive sampling minimizes the cost required for travel expenses (multiple round flight trips from the USA to Ethiopia) and other related expenses during data collection (Joyner et al., 2018). Though the study area was purposively selected, all depositors, loanees, and employees' data points of the relevant variables of the loan repaid (LNRD), operational self-sufficiency (OSS), return on asset (ROA), and business process (BP) from 2019 to 2023 was included for better statistical precision and to avoid potential errors due to the selection of a non-random sampling technique. As the number of clients and employees fluctuates from 2019 to 2023, the study considered all data points across the nineteen quarters for the selected variables. Employing all data points across the quarters from 2019-2023 in an inclusive way can minimize any potential sampling error and bias (Bhardwaj, 2019).

The study did not consider the remaining 16 districts of Omo Bank. However, the study covers all ten branches of Omo Microfinance under the Gofa zonal administration. The result's credibility was kept as all data points were considered in the study from 2019 to 2023 (Campbell et al., 2020). As the Sawla District Omo Bank is among the banks that implemented the modern internal banking system, the findings represent the financial and non-financial trends of Sawla Omo Bank. As a result, the study's findings do not represent the entire districts of Omo Bank (Andrade, 2021). As the study employed non-probability sampling of purposive sampling, the result of the study solely represents the Omo bank trend and may not apply to other industries. Such a problem of external validity is prevalent in almost all studies using non-probable sampling techniques (Egami

& Hartman, 2022). However, the findings represent branches under the Sawla District Omo Bank. Since the study does not employ a survey approach to data collection, the available quarterly and annual datasets from 2019 up to 2023 were considered.

Ethical Research

The participant branches and districts were selected based on the full voluntariness of managerial bodies. The required code of ethics of research and the institution was protected. The manager and relevant bodies providing the dataset signed a voluntary agreement to participate in the research and signed an informed consent form. The data collected from the district were retained and analyzed as part of the study results unless the participant institution requested the data to be destroyed. The study is for academic purposes and has no funding, so the participants had no financial incentive. To ensure the participant institution's ethical protection, informed consent and confidentiality of participant personal information were preserved in addition to other ethical standards of research (NCBI, 1979). The signed informed consent form is included. The consent form verifies how the research was based on the voluntariness of the participant organization and the manager working in the study area. The data would be securely kept confidential for five years (Xu et al., 2020).

Research ethics' baselines are privacy, confidentiality, and anonymity (Holland, 2019). Hence, for this study, personal identifying information was private. Identifying information of depositors and loanees was coded accordingly in the data management prior to analysis. The Omo Bank's internal database includes comprehensive customer details, so only relevant information was considered for the study. Sensitive information details were communicated via encrypted email to preserve the customers' operational and financial data confidentiality under Sawla District Omo Bank. Identifiers of organizations and customers in the study area were not collected and were kept anonymous (Holland, 2019).

Data Collection Instruments

The study used unpublished data from the quarterly financial and operational reports. The internal banking system of Omo Bank was the data source for the study. Kornegay and Segal (2013) claim that using observational data and existing data in combination increases the efficiency and power of research. However, the study was limited to using existing operational and financial data. The study employed latent and observed variables. While the latent variables are not directly measured as the observed variables, the former constructs are calculated based on observed variables (Kline, 2023). The measurement scale for most of the observed variables is expressed in ratios. Ratio scales are appropriate for data analysis in correlational studies (Acock, 2013; STATA, 2021). The latent and observed variables, the description of each variable, and the respective measurement approach are explained below. The practice of measuring each variable is based on the scholarly supported peer-reviewed article in chapter 2 of the literature review. Alternative measures were used based on the district's internal banking database data.

Observed variable: *Operating self-sufficiency (OSS)*: the ratio of the total operating income to operating expense. OSS is commonly used to measure self-sufficiency in banking industries (Ledgerwood, 1998).

Latent Variables and their Measure in Observed Variables

The Financial dimension of BSC(FP) is measured by Return on Asset (ROA). The ratio

of net income to the total asset is a measure of ROA (Frisch, 2014)

The Customer dimension of BSC(CS) is measured by Customer Retention (CR). The

number of loanees or voluntary depositors measures CR (Refera, 2020).

The Internal Business Process (BP) Dimension of BSC is measured by Borrowers(B) per

the number of Loan Officers (LnO) (Ali et al., 2020).

Learning and Growth Dimension of BSC(LG): measured by Employee Turnover Rate

(ETR)

ETR is the ratio of employees who left the company to the current employees working

actively in the Sawla District Omo Bank (Gautier et al., 2022).

Corporate Social Responsibility (CSR) is measured by the proxy measure of Financial

and Social Inclusion (FSI). The percentage of the women population counts FSI served in

financial and social inclusion (Gallego-Sosa et al., 2021).

The Business Agility (BA) dimension is measured by Cash Flow (CF). CF is Current

Asset (CA) minus Current Liabilities (CL) (Smart et al., 2019; Stobierski, 2020).

The Lean Banking (LB) dimension is measured by the Cost-to-Income Ratio (CIR) and

Operational Efficiency (OE). OE is measured by the proxy measure of the percentage of

loans repaid (LR) (Domenech et al., 2020; Mankins, 2017).

Table 2.

Latent and Observed Variables

No	Latent Unobserved Variables	Observed Variables	Proxy Measures of Latent Variables in Terms of Observed Variables	Independent Variable (IDV)/Dependent Variable (DV)	Hypothesized Correlation	References	Proposed Variables in Data Collection
1	Balanced Scorecard (BSC) Dimensions						
1.1	Financial(F)	Operating Self-Sufficiency (OSS), Return on Asset (ROA)	(i).OSS=Operating Income (OpY)/Operating Expense (OpEx) (Where OpY=Total Revenue (TRv)-Operating Expense (OpEx) (ii). ROA=Net Income (NtY)/Total Asset (TAst)	OSS: DV ROA: IDV	Positive (+ve)	(Kaplan & Norton, 1992; Ledgerwood ' 1998; Berman et al., 2013; Frisch, 20 14)	Total Revenue (TRv), Operating Expense (OpEx), Total Asset (TAst) & Net Income (NtY)
1.2	Customer (CS)	Number of Depositors (CSSV) and Number of Loanee (CSLn)	CSSV & CSLn	IDV	Positive (+ve)	(Kaplan & Norton, 1992; Refera, 2020)	Number of Depositors (CSSV) & Number of Loanee (CSLn)
1.3	Business Process (BP)	Number of New Borrowers (B) & Number of Loan Officers (LnO)	BP=B/LnO	IDV	Positive (+ve)	(Kaplan & Norton, 1992; Refera, 2020)	Number of New Borrowers (B) & Number of Loan Officers (LnO)
1.4	Business Learning and Growth (BLG)	Employment Turnover Rate (ETR)	ETR=Number of Employees Left (EmpLv)/Number of Active Employees (AcvEmp)	IDV	Negative (-ve)	(Kaplan & Norton, 2007; Refera, 2020; Kaplan & McMillan, 2021)	Number of Employees Left (EmpLv) & Number of Active Employees (AcvEmp)

No	Latent Unobserved Variables	Observed Variables	Proxy Measures of Latent Variables in Terms of Observed Variables	Independent Variable (IDV)/Dependent Variable (DV)	Hypothesized Correla tion	References	Proposed 15 Variables in Data Collection
2	Corporate Social Responsibility (CSR)	Number of Women Loan Beneficiaries (WPn)	WPn	IDV	Positive (+ve)	(Bowen, 1953; 2013; Carroll, 1979; 2018; 2021; Khursheed et al., 2021; Okesina, 2021; Daher et al., 2022; Mengstie, 2022).	Number of Women Loan Beneficiaries (WPn)
3	Banking Agility (BA)	Cash Flow (CshF)	CshF=Current Asset (CA)-Current Liability (CL)	IDV	Positive (+ve)	(Teece, 1997; Smart et al., 2019; Stobierski, 2020; Aghina et al., 2021; Freakley & Donahue, 2022)	Current Asset (CA) & Current Liability (CL)
4	Banking Leanness (BL)	Loan Repaid (LnRd)	LnRd=Total Loan Repayment (RP)/Loan Portfolio (LP)	IDV	Positive (+ve)	(Womack & Jones, 1996; Womack et al., 2007; Karlan et al., 2016; Chong, 2021; Schlesinger, 2021; Endris, 2022).	Total Loan Repayment (RP) & Loan Portfolio (LP)

Data Collection Technique

Data mining and record review were the primary techniques to extract the existing data from the Omo Bank internal database and available quarterly and annual reports from 2019 to 2023. The data mining technique is appropriate since most databases have massive amounts of data that may not be relevant for research (Maryoosh & Hussein, 2022). Additional annual records of reports were used to extract comprehensive financial banking data if not included in the database system. As data preparation in data mining techniques needs skills in data cleaning, data integration, data selection, data transformation, and pattern evaluation, requesting the participation of managerial experts in the internal Omo banking system is vital (Jassim & Abdulwahid, 2021). Due to the complexity of managing multiple variables and data quality issues, some challenges related to the timely collection of existing data are expected. Before the correlational analysis and reporting, as in data mining, latent and observed variables data were classified, checked for missing data and outliers, and remedial measures were taken for potential violations (Jassim & Abdulwahid, 2021).

Data Analysis

The study is aimed at answering the following research question.

Research Question 1. What is the relationship between business agility (BA), lean banking (LB), CSR initiatives, and the four BSC dimensions?

After testing the existence of a relationship, the following second research question was answered.

Research Question 2. What is the strength and direction of a relationship between business agility (BA), lean banking (LB), CSR initiatives, and the four BSC dimensions?

The following correlational hypotheses were tested to answer the first research question.

Null hypothesis: There is no statistically significant correlation between business agility (BA), lean banking (LB), Corporate Social Responsibility (CSR) initiatives, and the four Balanced Scorecard (BSC) dimensions, as measured by Kendall's Tau correlation coefficient (τ) with a small or negligible effect size.

(Null hypothesis: H0: $\tau = 0$, effect size <= small or negligible)

Alternative hypothesis: There is a statistically significant correlation between business agility (BA), lean banking (LB), Corporate Social Responsibility (CSR) initiatives, and the four Balanced Scorecard (BSC) dimensions, as measured by Kendall's Tau correlation coefficient (τ) with a large effect size.

(Alternative hypothesis: Ha: $\tau \neq 0$, the effect size is large)

The following null hypothesis(H0) and alternative (Ha) hypotheses were tested to answer the second research question.

Null hypothesis (H0): The correlation between business agility (BA), lean banking (LB), Corporate Social Responsibility (CSR) initiatives, and the four Balanced Scorecard (BSC) dimensions is not positive and statistically significant, with no or negligible effect size.

(H0: $\tau \leq 0$, the effect size is small or non-existent)

Alternative hypothesis (Ha): The correlation between business agility (BA), lean banking (LB), Corporate Social Responsibility (CSR) initiatives, and the four Balanced Scorecard (BSC) dimensions is positive and significant, with a large effect size.

(H: $\tau > 0$, there is a significantly large effect size).

From the theoretical and empirical standpoint, business agility (BA), lean banking (LB), and CSR initiatives positively affect the four BSC dimensions. Besides, the four BSC dimensions mediate the relationship between BA, LB, CSR initiatives, and organizational performance (OSS).

Correlation analysis would be relevant to analyzing the relationship between business agility, leanness, and CSR initiatives to the four BSC dimensions. According to Karlan and Luca (2022), correlation analysis significantly contributes to answering predictive problems in business. In this research, identifying the relationship between the observed variables associated with the latent variable of business agility, leanness, and CSR initiatives and the four dimensions of BSC helps to determine whether to increase or decrease the achievement of the variable identified for better organizational performance. Besides, in such a non-experimental research design, correlation analysis is a baseline for undertaking any regression analysis. In the case of linear regression and path analysis of structural equation modeling, variables with high correlation values have a higher contribution to accuracy for predicting the influence of the identified variable on the overall performance of an organization (Senthilnathan, 2019). In path analysis of structural equation modeling, the main objective is to identify the correlation direction and strength of the relationship among variables under the study (Acock, 2013; Hadwiansyah & Latief, 2022; Jassim & Abdulwahid, 2021; Kline, 2023; Maryoosh & Hussein, 2022; STATA, 2021; Williams et al., 2018;). The selection of correlation analysis as part of the data analytics of the study is based on the research objective of identifying the relationship between business agility, leanness, and CSR initiatives and the four dimensions of BSC. As the study employed panel data, initially identifying the relationship between the variables would help future researchers further analyze the mediating and moderating effect of the variables and predict organizational performance (Li & Andersson, 2021).

Data cleaning and screening were used to check the data quality before the correlation analysis (Huxley, 2020). The data cleaning encompassed coding variables involved in the study, data inputting, and checking the data distribution. As part of detecting the distribution of the data for the selected variables, histograms were used. Using histograms helps to visualize and understand the normality and non-normality of the data distribution (Nuzzo, 2019). As the study employed a quantitative method, the values of variables under the study are also numerical. Hence, employing histograms is helpful to visualize how far the distribution is from normality and understand the variability of data points (Boels et al., 2019). The Shapiro-Wilk test was used to statistically examine the data distribution (King & Eckersley, 2019). As the study has nineteen quarterly data points from the recent five years, from 2019-2023, with a small sample size, the selection of the Shapiro-Wilk test is appropriate. However, the Kolmogorov-Smirnov test would not be used as the Kolmogorov-Smirnov test is suitable for large sample sizes. The normality assumption was tested by checking the value of test statistics (W) and p-value. The value of test statistics (W) in the Shapiro-Wilk test ranges from 0 to 1, 1 indicating that the sample quantiles are closer to the assumed standard quartiles. The null hypothesis of the normality hypothesis was rejected for p-values greater than 0.05. The normality assumption was not met for variables with a p-value less than 0.05. The test statistics (W) showed how the quantiles were fitted to normal quartiles, showing the nature of data distribution (Mishra et al., 2019).

Suppose the data was found to be non-normally distributed. In that case, a non-parametric correlation analysis approach was employed to check the direction and strength of the relationship between the selected variables under the study. If the normality assumption of data distribution is met, parametric correlation analysis could be used (Schober & Vetter, 2020; Sheskin, 2020). While parametric inferential statistics assume the sample is randomly selected from the total population, the non-parametric test does not follow the assumption of randomness (Schober & Vetter, 2020). Based on the data distribution, either a parametric Pearson's correlation or a non-parametric Kendall's Tau correlation test approach would be employed to test the association between the variables. Kendall's Tau correlation is an alternative non-parametric to Spearman's rank correlation. Looking at the absolute value of the correlation coefficients, correlation values in a range of 0.70 up to 1 ($+0.70 \leq \tau < +1.00$) are considered as a very strong correlation, 0.50 up to 0.70 ($+0.50 \leq \tau < +0.70$) are strong correlation, $+0.35 \leq \tau < +0.50$ are fair or moderate correlation; $+0.20 < \tau < +0.35$ is weak correlation and $0.20 \geq \tau \leq +0.20$ is a very weak or negligible correlation. The negative and positive signs of the correlation coefficients were used to test the direction of the relationship. Positive correlation coefficients reflect the direct relationship, while negative correlation coefficients inform the inverse relationship between the variables (Senthilnathan, 2019).

Study Validity

From an external validity point of view, the study's findings did not represent the general application of the relationship between the variables in the entire Omo bank since the study employed the purposive sampling procedure to choose the study area (Andrade, 2021). Such a problem of external validity is prevalent due to the characteristics of non-probable sampling techniques (Egami & Hartman, 2022). However, as the ten branches under the Sawla District Omo Bank were considered, the results represent the branches under the study area. To assure internal validity, reliable and valid measures of variables were used coincidentally with the theory of financial management, accounting, organizational performance, and strategic management. Appropriate statistical procedures, correlational research design, and quantitative research methods were used to report and analyze the findings accurately.

The study assumes a direct and positive relationship between business agility (BA), lean banking (LB), CSR initiatives, and the four BSC dimensions. However, type-I and type-II may exist due to effect size, sample size, and data variability (Frost, 2020). Frost (2020) has an analogy explaining type-I and type-II errors in hypothesis testing in simple terms. According to Frost (2020), the situation is a false positive or type-I error if an alarm rings without fire. Fire alarms ring when there is a fire and do not ring when there is none. If an alarm does not ring during a fire, the situation is a false negative or type-II error. Both errors harm empirical studies' analysis of findings, conclusions, and study validity. Type-I error prevails when the null hypothesis is rejected when it is accurate or has a significant relationship between variables, but the theory does not support the claim. Type-II error exists when the null hypothesis is not rejected, is false, or the relationship between variables is supported, but there is no significance (Frost, 2020).

When effect sizes are more extensive, there would be an error of randomness (Frost, 2020). The larger the sample size, the smaller the effect. If the data has high variability, the randomness of the sample does matter (Frost, 2020). Hence, remedial measures for type-I and type-II errors were used to draw valid conclusions. The analysis can be used for academic purposes. Such academic writing encompasses relevant statistical techniques helpful in drawing conclusions based on prevalent insight.

Contrary to opinion, analysis based on sample informs the reality and the context—such academic analysis is based on existing theories and prior empirical findings (Buckingham et al., 2019). As Buckingham et al. (2019) stated, analysis based on academic research provides an understanding of the relationship of variables under study in a comprehensive approach. In addition, as there would be variability of patterns of variables included in the study, an empirical analysis paves the way for approximate precision (Buckingham et al., 2019). The analysis would be released after publication to access recommendations for the institution. Research findings in academic papers inform how businesses operate, and potential business challenges and later suggest scientific recommendations (Porter et al., 2022). As recommendations in an academic paper are supported by statistical evidence, academic theory, and the existing context of the problem under study, the Omo Bank may find it relevant to make informed adjustments to the services and products supplied to depositors and loanees. The research report could be published in one of the peer-reviewed financial journals: Journal of Banking and Finance, Quantitative Finance, Corporate Finance, Financial Analysts Journal, Journal of Finance, and Academy of Management journal. Scholars and institutions can access the research report from the ProQuest database of the dissertation.

Transition and Summary

The study's quantitative research method employed a correlational research design. Chapter 3 of the study research method presents the research design, data collection approach, and method of data analysis. In chapter 3, the sampling technique, ethical considerations, and the study's internal and external validity are assessed. Chapter 4 of the following study presents the results.

Chapter 4: Results

This study aimed to test if a statistically significant relationship exists between business agility, lean banking, and corporate social responsibility to the four balanced scorecard dimensions: customer, financial, learning and growth, and business process. The study employed quantitative methodology and correlational research design. The organizational success of microfinance was measured by Operational Self-sufficiency (OSS), the proxy measure of the financial dimension of the balanced scorecard. The study aimed to analyze the role of business agility, lean banking, and corporate social responsibility in the growth and transition of microfinance industries from a micro-credit and saving institution to a corporate bank. Hence, the study identified results of the correlation of the proxy measure of banking agility (cash flow), lean banking (loan repayment), and corporate social responsibility (women's financial inclusion) to the proxy measures of the four balanced scorecard dimensions. Chapter 4 comprises the study's findings to answer the following two research questions and test the hypotheses.

Research Question 1. What is the relationship between business agility (BA), lean banking (LB), CSR initiatives, and the four BSC dimensions?

The following hypotheses were tested to answer research question 1.

H0: There is no statistically significant correlation between business agility (BA), lean banking (LB), Corporate Social Responsibility (CSR) initiatives, and the four Balanced Scorecard (BSC) dimensions, as measured by Kendall's Tau correlation coefficient (τ), with a small or negligible effect size. (Null hypothesis: H0: $\tau=0$, effect size $<=$ small or negligible)

Ha: There is a statistically significant correlation between business agility (BA), lean

banking (LB), Corporate Social Responsibility (CSR) initiatives, and the four Balanced

Scorecard (BSC) dimensions, as measured by Kendall's Tau correlation coefficient (τ),

with a large effect size.

(Alternative hypothesis: Ha: $\tau \neq 0$, the effect size is large). After identifying the existence

of the relationships, the following second research question was answered.

Research Question 2. What is the strength and direction of a relationship between

business agility (BA), lean banking (LB), CSR initiatives, and the four BSC dimensions?

The following hypothesis was tested to answer the second research question,

H0: The correlation between business agility (BA), lean banking (LB), Corporate Social

Responsibility (CSR) initiatives, and the four Balanced Scorecard (BSC) dimensions is

not positive and statistically significant, with no or negligible effect size.

(H0: $\tau \leq 0$, the effect size is small or non-existent)

Ha: The correlation between business agility (BA), lean banking (LB), Corporate Social

Responsibility (CSR) initiatives, and the four Balanced Scorecard (BSC) dimensions is

positive and significant, with a large effect size.

(H: $\tau > 0$, there is a significantly large effect size).

Lastly, Chapter 4 encompassed the analysis of the study in brief.

Data Collection

Corporate quarterly data of Sawla District Omo microfinance was collected from the existing internal database employing data mining and record review techniques. The study encompassed all recent quantitative operational and financial data points from 2019 to 2023. The Sawla Omo microfinance was purposively selected by employing purposive non-random sampling. There were 19 quarterly data points from 2019 up to 2023. The study encompassed the ten branches under the Sawla District Omo Bank. As the study used purposive sampling with a small sample size, the distribution of data for different variables included had mixed results: random and non-random data distribution.

The research data was mined by the bank manager working on the internal system of Sawla District Omo microfinance. As a data mining process, relevant data points for fifteen variables such as Total Revenue (TRv), Operating Expense (OpEx), Total Asset (TAst), Net Income (NtY), Number of Depositors (CSSV), Number of Loanee (CSLn), Number of New Borrowers (B), Number of Loan Officers (LnO), Number of Employees Left (EmpLv), Number of Active Employees (AcvEmp), Number of Women Loan Beneficiaries (WPn), Current Asset (CA), Current Liability (CL), Total Loan Repayment (RP) and Loan Portfolio (LP) were collected to measure the significant proxy measures of the latent variables of business agility, lean banking, and corporate social responsibility and the four balanced scorecard dimensions: customer, financial, learning and growth, and business process.

During the data cleaning process, missing values and errors in the data ranges of each variable were checked and fixed by crosschecking with the original data.

Operational and financial data from the internal system and quarterly operational reports from record review were integrated, transformed, and converted into a single dataset file in a readily available spreadsheet for data analysis and reporting. After collecting the data points, proxy measures were calculated. After measuring proxy measures for the significant latent variables, the data distribution of variables was tested employing descriptive and inferential statistics. As the collected dataset had no identifiers, such as the names of depositors, loanees, and employees, the analysis kept the anonymity principle and ethics of the research.

Reliability and Validity

The data points were mined from an internal database system and quarterly records of Sawla District Omo microfinance. Quarterly organizational data on relevant variables were collected for academic research with the willingness and voluntarism of the managerial body working in the banking industry of the study area. Since the study employed a non-random purposive sampling to select the study area, the findings only represent the ten branches of Sawla District Omo microfinance. Hence, the result did not represent the entire Omo Bank and other similar micro-credit and saving institutions, as there was no external validity, referring to the fact that the result is not generalizable to the general population. The raw data collected consisted of 19 quarterly data points for every 15 variables considered for calculating the proxy measures of 7 main latent variables. A total of 24 variables were collected in the 19 quarterly data, with 456 data points.

The following measures were taken to validate the data integrity. The value ranges of each variable were checked for accuracy. The unit of measurement for each data point across the variables and periods was made uniform and validated for data consistency; missing data points were cross-checked with the original data points in the internal database for data completeness. Data was collected from the institution with an encrypted email communication and password-protected Excel file to preserve data security. Existing raw data was received from the institution, and the researcher calculated proxy measures of latent variables using suggested formulas based on theories of business administration disciplines of finance, accounting, management, and economics. Histograms were used to test the distribution of the dataset for each primary variable, and a statistical Shapiro-Wilk test was employed to check the normality of the dataset. A non-parametric Kendall's Tau correlation test was employed as the dataset was found to be non-normally distributed, with a small sample size collected using a non-random purposive sampling to test the relationship between the variables involved in the study.

Data Analysis

The data analysis section of the study comprehended relevant summary statistics such as quartiles for checking the outliers and measures of central tendency and distribution to check the data distribution for each proxy measure variable of Corporate Social Responsibility (CSR), Business Agility (BA), Lean Banking (LB) and the four dimensions of Balanced Scorecard (BSC). The data distribution of variables OSS, ROA, CSSV, CSLn, BP, ETR, WPn, CshF, and LnRd was checked using a histogram with a corresponding assumed normal curve to identify approximately normally distributed, non-normally right and left skewed variables. Afterward, for statistical precision, the data normality of variables involved in the study was tested using the Shapiro-Wilk test as the data collected was non-random with a small sample size. After conducting the Shapiro-Wilk test, variables with P-values greater than 0.05, close to normality, and variables with P-values less than 0.05, whose distribution departs from normality, were identified. Subsequently, as the data was found to be non-normally distributed, Kendall's Tau Correlation test was employed to test the hypotheses about the existence of a significant relationship among CSR, BA, LB, and the four dimensions of BSC and for testing the direction and strength of the relationship.

Results

In this section of the study, the analysis findings are discussed. The findings on the statistical summary presented the results in compact tables of quartiles and measures of central tendency and distribution with respective interpretations. Besides the summary statistics, the data distribution for each variable was visualized using histograms and assumed normal curves. The data visualization, statistical summaries, and test statistics for distribution and correlation analysis reports were computed using the STATA 14.2 statistical software package. The data distribution was identified and interpreted according to the statistical analysis. The test statistics of distribution were computed using the Shapiro-Wilk test, and the result was defined. After identifying the data distribution, the hypotheses were tested, and the result was discussed based on the test statistics of Kendall's Tau Correlation Matrix.

Table 3.

Compact Table of Summary Statistics: Quartiles for Checking Outliers

No.	Variable	Minimum Lowest value (Lowest boundary of data)	1st quartile Value below 25% of the data	Median (2nd quartile) Middle value of the data	3rd quartile Value below 75% of data	Maximum Highest value (Upper boundary of data)	Range Maximum minus Minimum	Interquartile range (IQR) 3rd Quartile minus 2nd Quartile	Count	Lower Outlier (Threshold) 2nd Quartile-(IQR*1.5)	Upper Outlier (Threshold) 3rd Quartile-QR*1.5
1	OSS	-0.38	0.44	0.8	1.75	2.93	3.32	0.06	19	0.35	
2	ROA	-3.47	0	0.01	0.01	0.04	3.51	0.01	19	-0.015	0
3	CSSV	380,128.00	382,252.00	391,125.00	393,252.00	409,715.50	29,587.50	11,000	19	365,752	409.
4	CSLn	70,125.00	81,254.00	84,258.00	87,125.00	89,383.00	19,258.00	5871	19	72,447.50	95,93
5	BP	15.27	17.03	20.5	21.25	23.75	8.48	4.22	19	10.7	2
6	ETR	0.02	0.03	0.05	0.06	0.08	0.06	0.02	19	0	(
7	WPn	144.9	185.4	198.45	218.25	246.15	101.25	32.85	19	136.125	267.
8	CshF	14,600,000	44,700,000	61,800,000	87,700,000	103,000,000	88,600,000	43,000,000	19	-19,800,000	152,200
9	LnRd	0.1	0.11	0.12	0.12	0.13	0.03	0.01	19	0.095	0.1

Table 3 reflects the distribution and central tendency of the dataset collected for

nine variables: OSS, ROA, CSSV, CSLn, BP, ETR, WPn, CshF, and LnRd. The quartiles

and ranges explain the variation and dispersion of the data points for each variable

(Mishra et al., 2019). The minimum, maximum, and quartile data show that all except OSS and ROA have positive data points. However, the minimum financial ratio values of variables OSS and ROA are negative. Values for all the proxy measures of the four dimensions of BSC, business agility, lean banking, and corporate social responsibility, have a positive value of quartiles. Before analysis, scholars recommend checking for outliers in the dataset. One approach to detecting lower and upper outliers is using interquartile ranges (Albert & Tullis, 2022). As shown in Table 3, all variables were found to have upper and lower outliers. As the data encompassed only 19 quarters of data points for each variable, with such a small sample size, removing the outliers may affect the correlation result. Besides, removing outliers may impact the result since the outliers represent a valid and meaningful trend of the variables selected.

Table 4.

Compact Table of Summary Statistics: Measures of Central Tendency and Dispersion

No.	Variable	Median	Mean	Variance	Standard Deviation (SD)	Coefficient of variation	Std e of m
		Middle value of the data	Average value of data	Deviation from mean	Average Deviation from Mean	SD/Mean	SD/s)
1	OSS	0.44	0.97	0.84	0.91	0.94	
2	ROA	0.01	-0.17	0.64	0.80	-4.65	
3	CSSV	391,125.00	390,863.82	60,600,000	7782.31	0.02	178
4	CSLn	84,258.00	82,639.11	36,500,000	6038.97	0.07	138
5	BP	20.50	19.32	6.82	2.61	0.14	
6	ETR	0.05	0.05	0.00	0.01	0.32	
7	WPn	198.45	201.62	602.13	24.54	0.12	
8	CshF	61,800,000	63,000,000	859,000,000,000,000	29,300,000	0.47	6,720
9	LnRd	0.12	0.12	0.00	0.01	0.06	

Table 4 exhibits the measures of central tendency: median and mean. Mishra et al. (2019) state that the median and mean denote the entire data distribution as the measures of dispersion calculated based on the mean value. On average, within the five-year interval from 2019-2023 of Sawla District Omo Bank, the Operational Self Sufficiency (OSS) is 0.44. As the average operational self-sufficiency is less than one, the study area could not cover its operating expenses. Future researchers can identify the root cause for deficiency in the Operational self-sufficiency of the institution, either checking for the impact of financial shock due to COVID-19 and the money market or the share company's long-run and short-run mission. On average, the Return on Asset, the relative profitability from its asset, is -0.17. The negative result indicates the challenge to make a profit from its assets. Individual data points for variables ETR and LnRd are negligible. However, the average deviation of data points from the mean for variables CSSV, CSLn, and CshF is larger, indicating a variability or dispersion in the dataset. Instead of removing outliers as a data cleaning and remedial measure of large data dispersion, the alternative robust correlation to Spearman correlation, Kendall rank correlation, is used in the analysis.

Distribution of the Data

Histograms are helpful to visualize how the data is distributed. Due to the normality assumption in parametric analysis, understanding how far the actual data is close or far from normal distribution can be checked by a histogram visual graph with a normal curve or testing for normality for objective determination of the data distribution. Histograms are beneficial for understanding the variability of the data (Boels et al., 2019;

Nuzzo, 2019). As the data points for the variables are continuous, the histograms are appropriate graphics. Based on STATA 14.2 data visualization result and the compact table summary statistics, variables Employment Turnover Rate (ETR) and Loan Repaid (LnRd) had a mean equal to the median and are approximately normally distributed variables, as shown in Figure 2. However, variable Operating Self-Sufficiency (OSS), the Number of Women Loan Beneficiaries (WPn), and Cash Flow (CshF) were found to have their mean greater than the median and are right or positively skewed. Contrarily, the variable Return on Asset (ROA), Number of Depositors (CSSV), Number of Loanee (CSLn), and proxy variable of business process (BP) were found to have their median greater than their mean and are left or negatively skewed as shown in Figure 4. Based on the data visualization by the histogram, all variables except the Employment Turnover Rate (ETR) and Loan Repaid (LnRd) have a non-normal distribution.

Figure 2.

Approximately Normally Distributed Variables

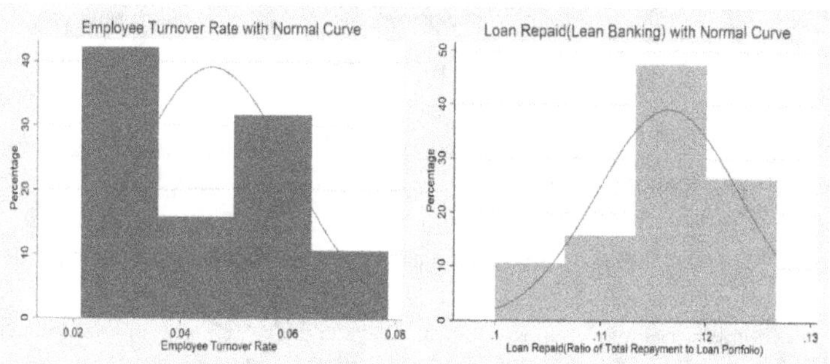

Figure 3.

Non-Normal Variables: Right Skewed

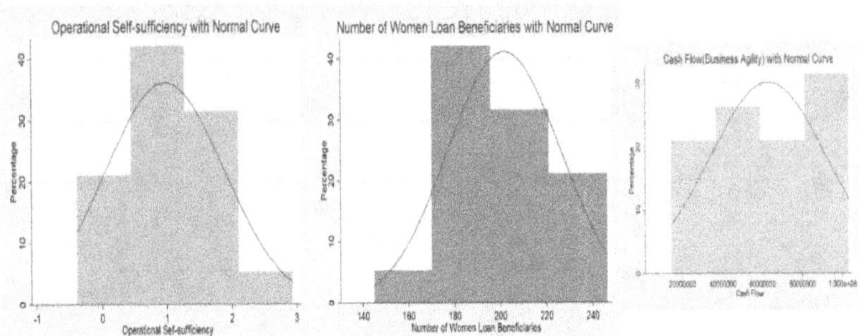

Figure 4.

Non-Normal Variables: Left Skewed

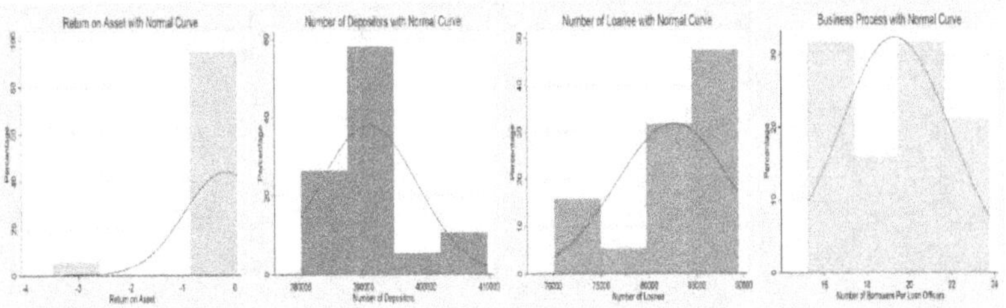

Table 5.

Shapiro-Wilk Test for Normal Data

No.	Variable	Observation	W (value of test statistics)	P-value
1	OSS	19	0.95	0.48
2	ROA	19	0.25	0.00
3	CSSV	19	0.90	0.04
4	CSLn	19	0.84	0.00
5	BP	19	0.94	0.23
6	ETR	19	0.96	0.55
7	WPn	19	0.97	0.83
8	CshF	19	0.93	0.16
9	LnRd	19	0.93	0.16

Table 5 presents the number of observations, the value of test statistics, and the p-value for the Shapiro-Wilk test. Objective test statistics are preferred to check normality than using visual histograms. Hence, the Shapiro-Wilk test was used as scholars prefer to use it with a small sample size (Mishra et al., 2019). In the Shapiro-Wilk test, the null hypothesis is that there is no distinction between the distribution of the data for the variables computed and a normal distribution. The alternative hypothesis is that there is a difference between the distribution of the data and a normal distribution. All except for variables Return on Asset (ROA), Number of Depositors (CSSV), and Number of

Loanees (CSLn) were found to have P-values greater than 0.05. Based on the Shapiro-Wilk test performed, the result did not show evidence of non-normality for the variable Operating Self-Sufficiency (OSS), the proxy variable of business process (BP), Employment Turnover Rate (ETR), Number of Women Loan Beneficiaries (WPn), Cash Flow (CshF) and Loan Repaid (LnRd) as the P-value was found to be greater than 0.05. However, as the variable Return on Asset (ROA), Number of Depositors (CSSV), and Number of Loanees (CSLn) were found to have P-values less than 0.05, the distribution for the variables departs from normality. Hence, Kendall's Tau non-parametric correlation, an alternative to Spearman's rank correlation, was used because some variables were not normally distributed based on the output from the Shapiro-Wilk test. As Kendall's Tau correlation does not assume a linear relationship between variables, this analysis does not include a scatterplot with the best-fit line. Note that ** ** $p \leq 0.0001$, *** $p \leq 0.001$, ** $p \leq 0.01$ and * $p \leq 0.05$.

Table 6.

Kendall's Tau Correlation Matrix

N o.	Variab les	OSS	ROA	CSSV	CSLn	BP	ETR	WPn	CshF	LnR d
1	OSS	-								
2	ROA	0.1243	-							
3	CSSV	-0.1243	(0.5266)**	-						
4	CSLn	-0.2059	0.1941	(0.3941)*	-					
5	BP	0.3068	-0.1180	-0.0944	-0.3050	-				
6	ETR	(0.4491)**	-0.0898	-0.2216	(-0.3989)*	(0.6568)***	-			
7	WPn	0.0118	(0.5782)***	(0.6962)***	(0.3636)*	0.0941	-0.0836	-		
8	CshF	-0.0765	(0.3471)*	(0.3824)*	-0.0175	-0.2346	-0.1369	0.2463	-	
9	LnRd	0.2765	-0.0059	-0.2412	(-0.5439)**	(0.4106)*	(0.5418)**	-0.1173	0.0409	-

Testing for Existence of Significance

A Kendall's Tau Correlation was performed to determine a correlation between business agility (BA), lean banking (LB), Corporate Social Responsibility (CSR) initiatives, and the four Balanced Scorecard (BSC) dimensions. The following hypotheses were considered to test the existence of a significant correlation.

Null hypothesis: There is no statistically significant correlation between business agility (BA), lean banking (LB), Corporate Social Responsibility (CSR) initiatives, and the four Balanced Scorecard (BSC) dimensions, as measured by Kendall's Tau correlation coefficient (τ) with a small or negligible effect size.

(Null hypothesis: H0: $\tau=0$, effect size <= small or negligible)

Alternative hypothesis: There is a statistically significant correlation between business agility (BA), lean banking (LB), Corporate Social Responsibility (CSR) initiatives, and the four Balanced Scorecard (BSC) dimensions, as measured by Kendall's Tau correlation coefficient (τ) with a large effect size.

(Alternative hypothesis: Ha: $\tau \neq 0$, the effect size is large)

As indicated in Table 6, the result revealed a significant correlation between the proxy measure of Corporate Social Responsibility (CSR), i.e., Number of Women Loan Beneficiaries (WPn), and the financial proxy dimension of BSC, i.e., Return on Asset (ROA), as shown by Kendall's Tau coefficient ($\tau=0.5782$, $p\leq0.0001$). Besides, the finding revealed that the Number of Women Loan Beneficiaries (WPn) had a significant correlation with the customer dimension of Balanced Scorecard (BSC), i.e., the Number of Depositors (CSSV) and Number of Loanees (CSLn) with Kendall's Tau coefficient ($\tau=0.6962$, $p\leq0.0001$) and ($\tau=0.3636$, $p\leq0.05$) respectively. The result shows that there is a significant relationship between CSR and the financial and customer dimensions of BSC. Contrarily, the result revealed no significant correlation between CSR and BSC dimension of Business Process (BP) and Business Growth and Learning (ETR). Simultaneously, contrary to the initial expectation, the result revealed that CSR was found to have no significant relationship with Operating Self-Sufficiency (OSS) with Kendall's Tau coefficient ($\tau=0.0118$). These results challenge the assumption that a significant correlation exists between CSR and Operating Self-Sufficiency (OSS) and need further study to identify factors that led to an unexpected relationship.

The finding showed a significant correlation between the proxy measure of Business Agility (BA), i.e., Cash Flow (CshF), and the financial dimension of BSC, i.e., ROA, and the customer dimension of BSC (CSSV) with Kendall's Tau coefficient (τ=0.3471, p≤0.05) and (τ=0.3824, p≤0.05) respectively. The result highlights the existence of a meaningful relationship between Cash Flow (CshF), Return on Asset (ROA), and the Number of Depositors (CSSV). Contradictory to the initial assumption, the proxy measure of Business Agility, i.e., Cash Flow (CshF), was found to have an insignificant correlation to Operating Self-Sufficiency (OSS) with Kendall's Tau coefficient (τ=-0.0765), which also needs further study in identifying the determining factors led to an unexpected finding.

The study revealed a significant correlation between the proxy measure of Lean Banking (LB), i.e., Loan Repaid (LnRd) and BSC dimension of Business Process (BP) with Kendall's Tau coefficient (τ=0.4106, p≤0.05). The finding informs the meaningful relationship between Loan Repaid (LnRd) and Business Process (BP). Besides, the result revealed a significant relation between the proxy measure of Lean Banking (LB), i.e., Loan Repaid (LnRd), the customer dimension of Balanced Scorecard (BSC), i.e., Number of Loanees (CSLn) and Learning and Growth (LG) dimension of BSC, i.e., Employee Turnover (ETR) with Kendall's Tau coefficient (τ=-0.5439, p≤0.01) and (τ=0.5418, p≤0.01) respectively. As in the case of the proxy measure of Corporate Social Responsibility (CSR) and Business Agility (BA), the proxy measure of Lean Banking (LB), i.e., Loan Repaid (LnRd), was found to have an insignificant correlation with the financial dimension of BSC, i.e., Operating Self-Sufficiency (OSS) with Kendall's Tau coefficient (τ=0.2765).

Testing for Direction and Strength of Relationship

Kendall's Tau Correlation was used to determine the direction and strength of the correlation between business agility (BA), lean banking (LB), Corporate Social Responsibility (CSR) initiatives, and the four Balanced Scorecard (BSC) dimensions. The following hypotheses were considered to test the direction and strength of the correlation. Null hypothesis (H0): The correlation between business agility (BA), lean banking (LB), Corporate Social Responsibility (CSR) initiatives, and the four Balanced Scorecard (BSC) dimensions is not positive and statistically significant, with no or negligible effect size.

(H0: $\tau \leq 0$, the effect size is small or non-existent)

Alternative hypothesis (Ha): The correlation between business agility (BA), lean banking (LB), Corporate Social Responsibility (CSR) initiatives, and the four Balanced Scorecard (BSC) dimensions is positive and significant, with a large effect size.

(H: $\tau > 0$, there is a significantly large effect size).

As shown in the Table. 4, the result revealed a strong positive correlation between the proxy measure of the Corporate Social Responsibility (CSR) variable, i.e., Number of Women Loan Beneficiaries (WPn), and the financial proxy dimension of the BSC variable, i.e., Return on Asset (ROA), as indicated by Kendall's Tau coefficient ($\tau=0.5782$, $p\leq0.0001$). The result indicates that as the Number of Women Loan Beneficiaries (WPn) increases, the Return on Asset (ROA) tends to increase. The positive value of Kendall's Tau coefficient(τ) indicates the direct association between the Number of Women Loan Beneficiaries (WPn) and Return on Asset (ROA), not necessarily a linear relationship. The effect size represented by Kendall's Tau coefficient of =0.5782 informs that changes in the Number of Women Loan Beneficiaries (WPn) are accompanied by the corresponding changes in Return on Asset (ROA) to a strong degree. In addition, the finding showed that the Number of Women Loan Beneficiaries (WPn) had a strong significant correlation with the customer dimension of Balanced Scorecard (BSC), i.e., the Number of Depositors (CSSV) with Kendall's Tau coefficient (τ=0.6962, p$\leq$0.0001). Since Kendall's Tau coefficient(τ) is found to be positive, the results imply a nonlinear direct relationship between the Number of Women Loan Beneficiaries (WPn) and the Number of Depositors (CSSV). The effect size 0.6962 shows a strong relationship between the variables and indicates that the change in the Number of Women Loan Beneficiaries (WPn) is strongly associated with the change in a positive direction of the Number of Depositors (CSSV). In addition, the finding revealed a significant moderate relationship between the Number of Women Loan Beneficiaries (WPn) and the Number of Loanees (CSLn) with Kendall's Tau coefficient (τ=0.3636, p$\leq$0.05). Consequently, as the proxy measure of Corporate Social Responsibility (CSR) has a direct significant relationship with BSC dimension financial variables of Return on Asset (ROA), and BSC customer dimension variables of Number of Depositors (CSSV) and the Number of Loanees (CSLn). Hence, the finding indicates that a change in the Number of Women Loan Beneficiaries (WPn) is accompanied by a positive change in Return on Asset (ROA), Number of Depositors (CSSV), and the Number of Loanees (CSLn).

The analysis revealed a positive moderate correlation between the proxy measure of Business Agility (BA), i.e., Cash Flow (CshF), and the financial dimension of BSC, i.e., ROA, and the customer dimension of BSC, i.e., the Number of Depositors (CSSV) with Kendall's Tau coefficient ($\tau=0.3471$, $p\leq0.05$) and ($\tau=0.3824$, $p\leq0.05$) respectively. The positive Kendall's Tau coefficients denote that as Cash Flow (CshF) increases, Return on Asset (ROA) and Number of Depositors (CSSV) increase nonlinearly. Kendall's Tau coefficients 471 and 0.3824 show a moderate effect size, suggesting that changes in Cash Flow (CshF) are accompanied by corresponding changes in Return on Asset (ROA) and Number of Depositors (CSSV) to a moderate degree.

The study confirmed a moderate positive correlation between the proxy measure of Lean Banking (LB), i.e., Loan Repaid (LnRd) and BSC dimension of Business Process (BP) with Kendall's Tau coefficient ($\tau=0.4106$, $p\leq0.05$). The positive Kendall's Tau coefficient of 0.4106 indicates the direct association between Loan Repaid (LnRd) and Business Process (BP). As Loan Repaid (LnRd) increases, the Business Process (BP) improves. In addition, the finding revealed a strong negative correlation between Loan Repaid (LnRd) and the Number of Loanees (CSLn) with Kendall's Tau coefficient ($\tau=-0.5439$, $p\leq0.0001$). The negative Kendall's Tau coefficient indicates the inverse association between Loan Repaid (LnRd) and the Number of Loanees (CSLn), implying that as the Loan Repaid (LnRd) increases, the Number of Loanees (CSLn) reduces. The finding yielded unexpected results, revealing a strongly positive correlation between the proxy measure of Lean Banking (LB), i.e., Loan Repaid (LnRd), and Learning and Growth (LG) dimension of BSC, i.e., Employee Turnover (ETR) with Kendall's Tau coefficient (τ=0.5418, p≤0.01). This unexpectedly strong positive relationship between Loan Repaid (LnRd) and Employee Turnover (ETR) challenges the initial assumption and needs further study to identify the leading factors of the relation.

Transition and Summary

Chapter 4 presented the analysis and result by first introducing how the data was collected and presenting the reliability and validity of the data. The result revealed a non-normal distribution of the data. As the study area and the quarterly recent data of 2019-2023 were purposively selected to understand how the Sawla District Omo microfinance transitioned from microfinance to a bank, the result is valid only for the study area involved. A non-parametric Kendall's Tau correlation test was employed due to the non-random nature of the data distribution. The study indicated a statistically positive significant correlation between Corporate Social Responsibility and the customer and financial proxy dimensions of BSC. The finding also identified a statistically positive significant correlation between the business agility proxy measure and the financial and customer dimension of BSC. Besides, the study revealed a statistically significant positive correlation between the lean banking proxy measure and the business process and growth and learning dimension of BSC. However, the study identified no statistically significant correlation between proxy measures of Corporate Social Responsibility, Business Agility, Lean Banking, and Operating Self-sufficiency. Chapter 5 presents the findings' interpretation, limitations of the study, applications to professional practice, and recommendations for action and further research.

Chapter 5: Discussion, Conclusions, and Recommendations

Interpretation of the Findings

The purpose of the study was to test if there exists a statistically significant correlation between the proxy measures of Business Agility (BA), Lean Banking (LB), Corporate Social Responsibility (CSR), and the four dimensions of the Balanced Scorecard (BSC). Besides, the study aimed at checking the strength and direction of the relationship between the selected continuous variables of Operating Self-Sufficiency (OSS), Return on Asset (ROA), Number of Depositors (CSSV), Number of Loanee (CSLn), Business Process (BP), Employment Turnover Rate (ETR), Number of Women Loan Beneficiaries (WPn), Cash Flow (CshF), and Loan Repaid (LnRd). The variables Operating Self-Sufficiency (OSS) and Return on Asset (ROA) were used as the proxy measures of the financial dimension of BSC. The variables Number of Depositors (CSSV) and Number of Loanees (CSLn) represented the customer dimension of BSC. The variable Business Process (BP) dimension of BSC was computed based on the ratio of new total loan beneficiaries per the number of loan officers. Employment Turnover Rate (ETR) was used as a proxy measure of the learning and growth dimension of BSC. Number of Women Loan Beneficiaries (WPn), Cash Flow (CshF), and Loan Repaid (LnRd) were used as the proxy measures of Corporate Social Responsibility (CSR), Business Agility (BA), and Lean Banking (LB), respectively.

Descriptive summary statistics of quartiles were computed to check the outliers. In addition, the central tendency and dispersion measures were computed to understand the distribution of nine variables employed in the test statistics. Histograms with the normal curve were also employed to visually understand how far the data points for each variable were from the assumed normal curve. The Shapiro-Wilk test was computed to check the normality of the data. The finding of the Shapiro-Wilk test revealed that variables Return on Asset (ROA), Number of Depositors (CSSV), and Number of Loanees (CSLn) were found to have P-values less than 0.05, which indicated non-normality. Since the summary statistics and the Shapiro-Wilk test confirmed the absence of normality in the data set, a non-parametric Kendall's Tau correlation test was used to decide on the null hypotheses of existence of significant relationship among the variables and to detect the strength and direction of the relationship between the proxy measures of Business Agility (BA), Lean Banking (LB), Corporate Social Responsibility(CSR), and the four dimensions of the Balanced Scorecard (BSC). Kendall's Tau correlation test implies the nonlinear relationship between the variables under study, unlike the linear relationship between variables under the Pearson correlation, which was determined due to the non-normal data distribution. The P-values of $p \leq 0.0001$, $p \leq 0.001$, $p \leq 0.01$, and $p \leq 0.05$ were used to test the existence of Kendall's Tau correlation. The positive and negative direction of the relationship between the variables was determined from the value of Kendall's Tau coefficient (τ). The strength of the correlation was realized after computing the absolute value of Kendall's Tau coefficient (τ). Variables with Kendall's Tau correlation coefficient (τ) absolute values in a range of 0.70 up to 1 ($+0.70 \leq \tau < +1.00$) were reflected as very strong correlation. Variables with Kendall's Tau correlation coefficient (τ) absolute values ranging from 0.50 up to 0.70 ($+0.50 \leq \tau < +0.70$) showed a strong correlation, while values 0.35 up to ($+0.35 \leq \tau < +0.50$) showed fair or moderate correlation. However, variables with Kendall's Tau correlation coefficient (τ) absolute values from 0.20 up to 0.35 ($+0.20 < \tau < +0.35$) and 0.20 up to 0.20 ($0.20 \geq \tau \leq +0.20$)

implied a weak and a very weak or negligible correlation.

Key Findings

Kendall's Tau correlation was tested, and the results of P-values of $p \leq 0.0001$,

$p \leq 0.001$, $p \leq 0.01$, and $p \leq 0.05$ were identified to understand whether the proxy measures

of the variables have a statistically significant correlation to answer the research question

of what is the relationship between business agility (BA), lean banking (LB), CSR

initiatives, and the four BSC dimensions. Note here that the four main variables, business

agility (BA), lean banking (LB), CSR initiatives, and the four BSC dimensions, were

considered as the multidimensional success metrics of organizational performance of the

banking industry. Kendall's Tau correlation coefficient (τ) was used to answer the

research question of the strength and direction of a relationship between business agility

(BA), lean banking (LB), CSR initiatives, and the four BSC dimensions. Positive

Kendall's Tau correlation coefficient (τ) implied the direct nonlinear correlation, while

negative Kendall's Tau correlation coefficient (τ) reflected the negative nonlinear

relationship between the variables. The absolute value of Kendall's Tau correlation

coefficient (τ) was used as the framework to determine if there existed a very strong,

strong, moderate, and weak strength of association between the proxy measures and

variables under the study.

Relationship Between the Proxy Measures of CSR And BSC Dimensions

Testing for the hypothesis of whether there was a significant statistical Kendall's

Tau nonlinear relationship between the proxy measures of CSR initiatives and the four

BSC dimensions, the study revealed a statistically significant correlation between the proxy measure of Corporate Social Responsibility (CSR), i.e., Number of Women Loan Beneficiaries (WPn), the financial proxy dimension of BSC, i.e., Return on Asset (ROA), and the customer dimension of Balanced Scorecard (BSC), i.e., the Number of Depositors (CSSV) and Number of Loanees (CSLn), nonlinearly. The finding confirms a nonlinear statistical relationship between the Number of Women Loan Beneficiaries (WPn), Return on Asset (ROA), Number of Depositors (CSSV), and Number of Loanees (CSLn).

Based on Bowen's (1953) and Carroll's (1979; 2021) theory of corporate social responsibility, banking enterprises are ethically responsible for empowering women and vulnerable parts of the community. Bowen (1953) and Carroll (1979; 2021) supported the idea that corporate banks should contribute economically to the community. However, Bowen (1953) and Carroll (1979;2021) did not further examine the contribution of CSR to an institution's overall organizational performance and success. After identifying a significant relationship between WPn, ROA, CSSV, and CSLn, the direction and strength of the nonlinear relationship was tested. Accordingly, the result confirmed a significant direct nonlinear relationship between WPn, ROA, CSSV, and CSLn. As previous studies by Bhatia and Singh (2019) confirm an indirect relationship between CSR and organizational performance and success, the findings coincide with the theory of CSR and empirical studies of Bhatia and Singh (2019). Hence, this study is an eye-opener to understand how CSR can contribute to organizational performance. Based on the findings, the participation of Sawla District Omo Bank in the financial inclusion of women or CSR initiative had an association with an indirect nonlinear increase of ROA and the total number of depositors and the loanees, which is the customer dimension of

BSC. However, the study disconfirmed the existence of a significant relationship between CSR, the financial dimension of BSC, i.e., Operating Self-Sufficiency (OSS), the Business Process (BP) dimension of BSC, and Business Growth and Learning (ETR). The unexpected result that WPn, i.e., CSR proxy measure, had no significant nonlinear relation with Operating Self-Sufficiency (OSS) needs further research to examine contributing factors for the absence of a relationship.

Relationship Between the Proxy Measures of Business Agility and BSC Dimensions

As the data was found to be non-normally distributed, Kendall's Tau correlation test was executed to check if a nonlinear correlation exists between the proxy measure of Business Agility (BA), i.e., Cash Flow (CshF), and the four dimensions of BSC. The result revealed a significant nonlinear correlation between Cash Flow (CshF), the financial dimension of BSC, i.e., ROA, and the customer dimension of BSC (CSSV). The study confirmed a moderate nonlinear positive correlation between CshF, ROA, and CSSV testing for the direction and strength of the nonlinear correlation between the proxy measures. Based on Teece et al. (1997) theory of dynamic capabilities and strategic management, there should be sufficient cash flow to build internal capability in an ever-changing agile business environment. Teece et al. (1997) previously had not examined which performance metrics were associated with cash flow, a proxy measure of Business Agility (BA). However, Aghina et al. (2021) stated that the customer dimension of BSC and financial health had a direct relationship. Hence, the finding that CshF, ROA, and CSSV had a positive direct nonlinear relationship coincides with the theory of business agility by Teece et al. (1997) and the study by Aghina et al. (2021). However, the study disconfirms the correlation between business agility and OSS, one of the financial dimensions of BSC, which calls for future investigation on understanding and determining factors that led to no relation between cash flow and OSS.

Relationship Between the Proxy Measures of Lean Banking and BSC Dimensions

Using Loan Repaid (LnRd) as the proxy measure of Lean Banking (LB), Kendall's Tau correlation was employed to answer the research question of the relationship between LB and the four dimensions of BSC. Based on the result P-value associated with Kendall's Tau test, the findings confirmed a statistically significant nonlinear relationship between Loan Repaid (LnRd), Business Process (BP), the customer dimension of Balanced Scorecard (BSC), i.e., Number of Loanees (CSLn) and Learning and Growth (LG) dimension of BSC, i.e., Employee Turnover (ETR). After testing for the strength and direction of the relationship between Loan Repaid (LnRd) and the BSC dimensions: Business Process (BP), Number of Loanees (CSLn), the finding revealed a direct strong relationship between Loan Repaid (LnRd) and Business Process (BP). However, Loan Repaid (LnRd) and the Number of Loanees (CSLn) had a strong negative nonlinear relationship.

Based on Womack & Jones's (1994) theory of lean management, needless steps of human capital and time should be reduced to optimize organizational performance and produce at least possibly cost and avoiding waste. Accordingly, the result coincides with the theory of lean management principle in that as the number of loanees increases, it affects the Loan Repaid (LnRd), which suggests managing loans appropriately. On the other end, following the lean management principle, as the Sawla District Omo Bank Loan Repaid (LnRd) increased, the result witnessed a nonlinear increase or improvement in the BSC dimension of Business Process (BP). As per the empirical evidence of research study by Karlan et al. (2016) and Schlesinger (2021), a Loan Repaid (LnRd) is considered a good indicator of banking performance. Contrary to theoretical assumptions and empirical studies, the study disconfirms the inverse relationship between the Loan Repaid (LnRd) and Learning and Growth (LG) dimension of BSC, i.e., Employee Turnover (ETR), which calls for further research to identify the factor that led to a positive nonlinear relationship. Besides, the study disconfirms a statistically significant relationship between OSS and Lean Banking (LB) proxy measure.

Limitations of the Study

The limitation of the study is related to the potential of the research finding external validity. The capability of the study to be generalized to the whole industry is affected by the nature of the data distribution, the sample size, and the research design employed to test the hypotheses (Ross & Zaidi, 2019). Since this study has considered a small sample employing non-random purposive sampling on the quarterly data of Sawla District Omo Bank, the findings only represent the prevalence of the relationship of the selected variables in the study area within the year 2019-2023. However, as the data has not included all districts under Omo Bank, the result does not represent excluded districts and branches of Omo Bank and other rival competitive banks in Ethiopia. Due to the non-normal distribution of the data, the result of Kendall's Tau correlation does not reflect a linear correlation between the selected variables but instead indicates a nonlinear relationship. The study is not experimental, so Kendall's Tau correlation test findings do not reflect causation (Rohrer, 2018). Hence, the study result may not apply to similar micro-credit, microfinance, and shareholder banks.

Applications to Professional Practice

As the study examined the relationship between proxy measures of business agility, corporate social responsibility, lean banking, and the four dimensions of the balanced scorecard, the findings are relevant to understanding the prevalent situation of financial metrics positively and negatively associated with organizational multidimensional performance metrics and to understand emerging variables influencing the success of banking sector, particularly to identify variables contributing to the transition of microfinance to banks. The findings and insights inform the institution to work on performance metrics if Sawla Omo Bank aims to boost business agility, lean banking, or corporate social responsibility and compete in the money market.

Since organizational success cannot be achieved by working on a single operational or financial dimension of the banking sector, similar financial institutions can learn how cash flow boosts business agility and loan repayment indirectly contributes to lean management. Simultaneously, nowadays, businesses compete to get fame in achieving a better performance in corporate social responsibility. Such a run has significantly contributed to attracting customers and keeping the brand of banks and firms. The findings potentially suggest pathways to optimizing social responsibility performance. Hence, the institution now has relevant information on how working on business agility, lean banking, and corporate social responsibility influences the operational and financial performance of the bank. From an ethical perspective, working on corporate social responsibility initiative not only contribute to the depositors and beneficiaries of loan distribution but also enhance organizational performance, simultaneously attracting customers and improving the return on asset of the financial institutions.

Implications for Social Change

The primary purpose of this study was to understand how Sawla District Omo Bank transitioned from microfinance to a bank. The research findings on the statistically significant relationship between the proxy measures of business agility, lean banking, corporate social responsibility, and the four balanced scorecard financial and non-financial dimensions inform the business sectors on how to be exemplary and achieve improved organizational performance. Nowadays, businesses should not run solely to optimize financial profitability. The finding in the study informs how banking industries and financial institutions can simultaneously achieve objective financial and non-financial organizational performance by working on their ethical and economic responsibility to the community.

The study can also inform how a culture of participating in social corporate responsibility benefits institutions and the community. Organizational performance can be achieved by designing appropriate strategic management plans and mitigating risk factors tackling the institution's performance. In contemporary business, corporate industries' organizational performance and success are triggered by values and organizational culture. As the study identified emerging variables such as business agility, lean banking, and corporate social responsibility, the institution under the study should recheck and balance the values where each metric is based. The values and principles of the institution should accord and be improved to mitigate emerging challenges of future business shocks. Preparing ahead of time would save the industry from unforeseen business liquidity and challenges. As microfinance industries are built to supply financial and saving services for a low-income and vulnerable part of the community, improving the customers' financial well-being contributes indirectly to organizational performance and community development.

Recommendations for Action

The study aimed to identify how business agility, lean banking, and corporate social responsibility are associated with organizational performance's financial and non-financial indicators of the banking sector, focusing on finding how microfinance industries can transition from a micro-credit and saving to a corporate bank. The study's recommendations could help financial analysts, strategic managers, and transformational leaders working in microfinance and corporate banks understand how financial ratios are directly and indirectly linked to banking performance in the money market. The following section states three main recommendations for action.

Scale Up Women's Financial Inclusion and Work on Savings for Financial Capability

The banking institution should work on scaling up women's financial inclusion, boosting the cash flow and loan repayment to compete in an agile business environment of the money market. The finding that women's financial inclusion as an initiative of corporate social responsibility, nonlinearly increasing the customer dimension of a balanced scorecard, informs how banking managers should realize the double-fold advantage of participating in social corporate performance. The banking institution should scale up initiatives and investments in social corporate responsibility to attract more customers. Simultaneously, as customer satisfaction and enrollment increase, the bank would have the potential to contribute to social responsibility and boost organizational performance. The result that cash flow is associated with return on asset and the number of depositors informs how banking officials should work on boosting the number of depositors to have a sufficient cash flow and returns and prepare for unforeseen challenges during financial shocks. The banking institution should work on saving mobilization to mitigate the emerging challenges. With a particular focus on voluntary saving and compulsory saving of loanees, the future financial well-being of the institution can be maintained.

Increase Loan Repayment for Improved Business Processes and Lean Management

The finding that loan repayment, the proxy measure of lean banking and management, has a positive association with business processes tells the institution to work on loan repayment for an improved business process and lean management. The finding indicates that higher loan repayment is associated with a higher business process improvement. Hence, the institution should minimize loans getting to arrears to minimize financial resource wastage leading to bankruptcy. Successful microfinance and banks have a high rate of loan repayment. Hence, the finding informs how arrears adversely affect the performance of business processes and overall organizational performance.

Disseminate The Research Result and Develop Scientific Approaches for Improved Performance

The banking institution should disseminate the research result to managerial bodies working in operation, finance, and strategic management, and the research and development department to make a better understanding of how financial inclusion of women, positive in and outflow of cash and loan repayment can improve and enhance the competitive capability of the institution in areas of business agility, lean banking and social corporate responsibility performance and the resulting association to multidimensional performance metrics of success. Apart from spreading the findings to officials and managerial bodies working in the industry, the corporate bank should develop scientific approaches to scale up performance in business agility and leanness and corporate social responsibility to undertake ethical and business responsibility for the mutual benefit of society and the bank.

Recommendations for Further Research

This study examined proxy measures of lean banking, business agility, and corporate social responsibility, which are nonlinearly associated with increasing banking performance's financial and non-financial dimensions, employing a quantitative research method and correlational research design. Future researchers could conduct extensive and in-depth research on the following aspects based on the research findings. The following section covers the three recommendations for further research.

Identify Uncovered Proxy Measures

This study identified proxy measures of business agility, lean banking, and corporate social responsibility solely focused on existing data gathered on financial and non-financial metrics. The metrics identified were cash flow, loan repayment, and women's financial inclusion in the bank. Future researchers could exhaustively review business agility, lean banking, and corporate social responsibility theories and identify uncovered alternative metrics in this study that may influence the banking industry's organizational performance. These measures could be collected using a survey method.

Expand Sample Size

This study used a non-random purposive sampling technique. The study employed quarterly data points from 2019-2023 with a small sample size to particularly understand if performance in business agility, lean banking, and corporate social responsibility is associated with an increase in financial and non-financial performance of the Sawla District Omo bank. The small sample, in turn, affected the distribution of the data type and the type of research design to be used in the analysis. Hence, future researchers could expand the sample size with a random selection of participants for better precision and conclusion and external validity of the research findings.

Use Experimental Research

This study used a non-experimental research approach to examine the association between proxy measures of business agility, lean banking, and corporate social responsibility and the four dimensions of the balanced scorecard. As this study already examined the proxy measures associated with each banking performance and their respective correlation, future researchers could precisely measure the contribution of women's inclusion in finance, loan repayment, and cash flow in realizing successful organizational performance using experimental research. Such experimental research may help understand each proxy measure's likelihood contribution, possibly employing tree analysis and predictive modeling using structural equations and other parametric analyses. Structural equation modeling may help future research further examine moderating and mediating factors that may influence the strength and direction correlation between the variables under the study.

Reflections

The Doctor of Business Administration study process has brightened my understanding of the association of business agility, lean management, and participating in corporate social responsibility initiatives and banking performance. The preconceived idea that business agility, lean management, and participation in corporate social responsibility initiatives have a direct and strong correlation with operational self-sufficiency was not proved in this study. The finding instead informed me that there is no single success metric to measure the organizational performance of the banking industry. Methodologically, the researcher's perspective on the small sample size and non-experimental research potential in building a predictive model changed as I delved into scholarly articles and worked on the data analysis.

Conclusion

This study examined the relationship between banking agility, leanness, and corporate social responsibility proxy measures and banking performance's financial and non-financial dimensions. The study revealed how women's inclusion in the financial initiative is associated with a nonlinear increase in saving and loan customer attraction and improvement in return on assets of the study area, employing a quantitative research method and non-parametric correlational research design. The study also showed how a positive cash flow is associated with the clients' saving behavior and a positive return on assets. In addition, the findings presented how loan repayment is associated with improved business processes. The findings are relevant to strategic managers working on improving banking industries' organizational performance. Future researchers and readers could get a background foundational knowledge by reviewing Chapter 1 on the problem of challenges of banks in achieving self-sufficiency and realizing multidimensional optimum successful organizational performance, Chapter 2 on theories and empirical research on banking agility, leanness, and corporate social responsibility and the four dimensions of the balanced scorecard, Chapter 3 on quantitative research method employed and the non-parametric correlational research design, Chapter 4 on results and Chapter 5 on discussion, conclusion, and recommendations.